BEYOUROWN CAREERCOACH

THE TOOLKIT YOU NEED TO BUILD THE CAREER YOU WANT

RUS SLATER

PEARSON

Harlow, England • London • New York • Boston • San Francisco • Toronto • Sydney
Auckland • Singapore • Hong Kong • Tokyo • Seoul • Taipei • New Delhi
Cape Town • São Paulo • Mexico City • Madrid • Amsterdam • Munich • Paris • Milan

PEARSON EDUCATION LIMITED

Edinburgh Gate
Harlow CM20 2JE
Tel: +44 (0)1279 623623
Fax: +44 (0)1279 431059
Website: www.pearson.com/uk

First published in Great Britain in 2012

ISBN: 978-0-273-77116-6

British Library Cataloguing-in-Publication Data
A catalogue record for this book is available from the British Library

Library of Congress Cataloging-in-Publication Data
A catalog record for this book is available from the Library of Congress

10 9 8 7 6 5 4 3 2 1
16 15 14 13 12

Cartoons by Bill Piggins
Typeset in 11pt Helevetica Neue Light by 30
Printed and bound in Great Britain by Henry Ling Ltd., at the Dorset Press, Dorchester, Dorset

PRAISE FOR *BE YOUR OWN CAREER COACH*

"*I have worked with Rus over the past three decades and he is one of*

02. APR 13.

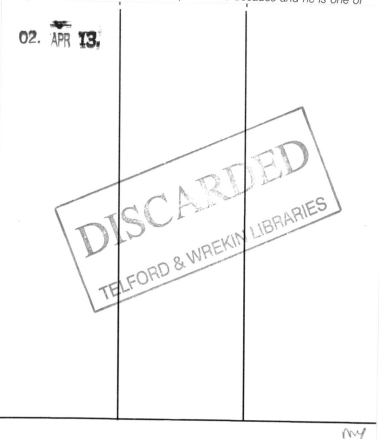

Please return/renew this item
by the last date shown.
Items may also be renewed by
Telephone and Internet.
Telford & Wrekin Libraries
www.telford.gov.uk/libraries

that makes the journey through the book a lot less daunting than it might be. Read it and reap!" GRAHAM O'CONNELL, HEAD OF LEARNING STRATEG

PEARSON

At Pearson, we believe in learning – all kinds of learning for all kinds of people. Whether it's at home, in the classroom or in the workplace, learning is the key to improving our life chances.

That's why we're working with leading authors to bring you the latest thinking and the best practices, so you can get better at the things that are important to you. You can learn on the page or on the move, and with content that's always crafted to help you understand quickly and apply what you've learned.

If you want to upgrade your personal skills or accelerate your career, become a more effective leader or more powerful communicator, discover new opportunities or simply find more inspiration, we can help you make progress in your work and life.

Pearson is the world's leading learning company. Our portfolio includes the Financial Times, Penguin, Dorling Kindersley, and our educational business, Pearson International.

Every day our work helps learning flourish, and wherever learning flourishes, so do people.

To learn more please visit us at: www.pearson.com/uk

Contents

About the author vi

Publisher's acknowledgements viii

Introduction ix

   How to use this book xii

1 Your life goals and your legacy 1

2 Your values and beliefs 17

3 Your likes and dislikes 33

4 Balancing your work and your life 53

5 What's your brand? 67

6 Family: fitting your lifestyle/career with theirs 81

7 Family *as* a career 89

8 The evolution of your career; can you future-proof it? 99

9 Soar with the egos 121

10 Putting it back 147

11 Learning and earning 155

12 Getting the word out there 171

13 Wage slave or captain of your own destiny? 179

Bibliography 198

Glossary 199

Index 201

About the author

RUS SLATER has been a career coach since the mid 1990s. His experience in this field has led him to work with people ranging from the unemployed (across the nation) to the General Secretary of a Trade Union, from people who are leaving school to people who are coming back out of retirement, and from people who are looking for a job to people who are setting up their own businesses.

He is also a 'portfolio' worker, and when he is not career coaching he designs and delivers management training programmes to organisations ranging from small local charities to global conglomerates. Some of this takes him to exciting, far-off venues such as High Wycombe and Chippenham, and some of it he delivers online by 'virtual classroom' from his dining room. He is also a volunteer 'lengthsman' on the local waterway and takes guests from the Hampshire Four Seasons Hotel on country walks.

He has changed career several times in his life, having worked in advertising and television, commanded a Troop of Royal Engineers in the British Army and been an HR manager.

Based on his experience he has written four internationally successful books: three in the *Business Secrets* series for HarperCollins and one to tie in to the hit BBC TV series

Dragons' Den.

He would like to dedicate this book to his wonderful wife, who has put up with it all (and, he hopes, will continue to do so!), even to the point of proofreading the manuscript of this book!

Publisher's acknowledgements

We are grateful to the following for permission to reproduce copyright material:

Cartoon on page 9 from www.CartoonStock.com; cartoon on page 36 with thanks to Theresa McCracken; text on pages 44–8 from AGCAS; extract on page 79 from Lucinda Slater's blog 'Communicating your brilliance'.

Every effort has been made to trace the copyright holders and we apologise in advance for any unintentional omissions. We would be pleased to insert the appropriate acknowledgement in any subsequent edition of this publication.

Introduction

When I left school in the late 1970s, 'career planning' was summed up by looking at milestones: 'If I join the management trainee scheme at Marks and Spencer, I'll be a store manager by the time I'm 25 and a regional manager by the time I'm 30'; 'If I join the RAF, I'll be a Squadron Leader by the time I hit 32'; 'I'm going to work at the Weetabix factory and I should make it through the apprenticeship and up to shift supervisor by the time I'm 35'.

Career planning was seen as a ladder-climbing activity, often with precious little thought as to what you'd actually be doing with your time 9 to 5, five days a week, 48 weeks a year, year after year . . .

Since then there has been a seismic shift in the world of work. As with everything, there are two sides to the story: the threats and the opportunities.

The threats

Long gone is the job for life – the paternal company nurturing your career and looking after you until you toddle off at around 65 with a nice carriage clock. Now we live in a world where jobs, teams and whole industries can disappear in a few years. The vast majority of us will face redundancy at some point in our careers and it is predicted that someone graduating this year will have had between 11 and 14 jobs by the time they hit their mid thirties.

The opportunities

No longer are we shackled to one company, industry and career path for our whole working lives. There is a vast range of opportunities open to us and we can work in many different ways and have many different careers.

The impact of all of this on you is that the onus has shifted from being employed to being employable. It is now down to you to manage your career. That means each and every one of us will constantly and consistently have to re-evaluate and re-assess our wants, desires, skills, attributes and options and make the most of them.

That is just what this book sets out to help you do. By being your own career coach you can be at the top of your game, open to opportunities and ready to take advantage of the ones that suit you.

CASE STUDIES

Gordon was being made redundant from his role as a parts warehouseman in a large government-owned automotive repair workshop. It was the only job he had ever done in his entire life. He 'resettled' as a props manager for a television production company, using very similar skills.

Two sheet metalworkers from a company that made prosthetic limbs for amputees were put out of work by the change in their industry to 'beach-wear' artificial limbs . . . they set up a small business making vases and planters from recycled oilcans.

The book is for you if:

- your job has been made redundant and you want some guidance on next steps;
- you've been in one career for a while and want a change;
- you think your current career isn't sustainable in the future and want to examine your options;
- you've had a bit of a life-changing experience/reached a metaphorical crossroads and want to re-assess your life and re-align your future;
- you're just plain fed-up!
- you're curious about different types of working, such as freelancing, but don't want to take the leap before investigating the realities of life outside the corporate nest;
- you need to re-align your career to fit in with a significant other;
- you are returning to the world of work after a career break;
- your previous career was a first career but is not suitable for an older (or wiser) person (I'm not being ageist here, but thinking of people who, much as I did, might have spent some time in the military, for instance, but

recognised that, after many years, living in a hole in the ground has lost its attraction);

- you are just starting your career and don't want to end up doing something for a few years before realising it is the wrong path.

"The advice I got was to get a job, any job, because then I would get a foot on the work ladder. It was good advice, I could, like many contemporaries, have spent the next decade or two unemployed. It is so much easier, as they say, to get a job when you have a job." TERRY GEORGE, FREELANCE CONSULTANT

HOW TO USE THIS BOOK

I've written this book to help you towards having a happy and fulfilling work life, but its main purpose is not to spoon-feed you answers, after all there is no 'one size fits all' career plan. You are unique, with your own talents, dreams and ambitions, and this book is designed to work with those and ask you powerful and challenging questions to help you develop a bespoke plan that works specifically for you.

Although the questions are in the book, you're not answering to the book, nor indeed to anyone other than yourself. Please, therefore, remember that there is no right or wrong answer, there is no one that you have to please, nor any political or moral opinion with which you have to comply. For instance, the question may ask what is more important to you, your family or the amassing of material wealth. For many people in the post-credit-crunch, developed world of the twenty-first century, we would immediately answer that family was most important. However, if you genuinely feel that, for you, wealth is more important then go for it! The objective of the book is to help you to make your best decisions based on your needs, not to 'help' you to conform to the expectations of other people.

How you choose to answer the questions and consider the issues is again entirely up to you; you may simply muse on the topic as you commute to work or you may choose to set aside specific times to ponder the issues. You may just think or you may choose to actually write down your thoughts. Committing your goals, plans, aspirations and wants to the written word (whether in handwritten manuscript or electronic form) helps you not only to formulate your opinions in a rounded way but, later on, to look back and remind yourself of them and see how your attitudes have evolved over time.

A study by the Dominican University of California found that writing down your goals is a proven way of increasing the likelihood of seeing them through. It went on to show that if you write down your goals and then share them with a supportive friend, you increase the likelihood of success even more . . . it also suggested that if you then keep that supportive friend updated with progress reports you add an even greater success factor to achieving your goals. So, if you really want to get the maximum from your career and personal development you might want to find yourself a supportive friend or two with whom you can share your thoughts.

It doesn't have to be a formal relationship of mentor and student or shrink and patient, but more along the lines of Mick 'Crocodile' Dundee's question when someone mentions discussing your problems with a shrink, 'Hasn't she got any mates?'. A semi-casual conversation over a coffee followed by some progress report tweets is exactly the sort of 'supportive friend' relationship that works.

Alternatively, a lot of the scenario assignments you'll find in the book are the sort of conversation that you might well have in the pub with a friend or friends. You never know, the conversation may benefit them as well. Your discussion of your life goals, career plans, values and so on is likely to get your supportive friends thinking about their own situation, so the whole thing becomes a virtuous cycle of self-improvement.

A few words on the meaning of 'support'

There is an adage that 'When two people always agree, one of them is unnecessary when it comes to decision making'. This means that:

- A *supportive* friend is NOT the one who *always* agrees with you or *always* thinks that your ideas are great.

- A *supportive* friend would NOT go along with an idea, or give tacit approval to a plan, just to tell you, 'Oh, I could have told you that would happen', when you later fail.

- A *supportive* friend is NOT one who takes over your decisions and makes them for you (that is a control freak).

- A *supportive* friend is NOT someone who tells you how they did it back in the past and then expects you to copy their way . . . their way may have worked for them, then, in those historic circumstances, but they won't necessarily work for you, now, in your present environment. Likewise, a supportive friend will recognise that just because they tried something and it failed that doesn't mean that you can't achieve it; as the investment advisors should point out, 'Past performance is no guarantee of future results'.

A supportive friend will make *you* think things through by asking you questions such as:

- What might be the consequences of that?
- How difficult will that be to pull off?
- Who might help you with that?
- How might they be of help?
- How will you find them?
- What will you say to them?
- Why haven't you done anything yet?
- What else could you do/learn/plan in order to make it work?
- When will you do that?
- Who might be upset about that?
- How upset might they be?
- How much do you want it?
- What is stopping you?
- What effect might that have?
- How long will it take to start?
- How will you know it is working?
- How long will it take to succeed?
- What will success look like?

- What will you *do* if that doesn't work?
- How will you *feel* if it doesn't work?
- How much will you gain if it does work?
- How much will you lose if it doesn't?

This sort of questioning is helpful; it supports you by making you think through the idea fully before you get too tied up in it to extricate yourself without serious loss.

Sometimes a supportive friend, after asking you lots of questions, may feel the need to tell you their opinion . . . 'I think you are absolutely mad!'.

Remember that it is *your* choice to decide whether to listen to them or not . . . your career, your decisions. They are questions that only you can answer because they are questions that relate to you and your situation alone. You don't have to fall out with your mates over it, just agree to disagree.

If you'd rather not share it with a friend then have an 'internal dialogue' with yourself; ask yourself all the questions above. You don't need an imaginary friend, but learn to 'self-coach': ask yourself these questions and answer them to the absolute best of your ability.

One recommendation is to get yourself a hardback, lined book and use that to complete each activity in writing. Only write on the left-hand pages, leaving the right-hand pages blank. This will then be a document you can keep as you go through your life, adding to and annotating, using the space you left as you filled in the book. Imagine being able to refer back in the future to emulate your success, avoid repeating your mistakes and share your learning with your family or friends.

Sometimes you will be tempted to skip over one of the activities or challenges in this book. If you find yourself in this position that is not necessarily a problem; it is fine if you decide to skip sections so long as:

1 you give it some serious thought before you decide to skip it;

2 you skip an activity for a rational reason rather than because it is just easier in the short term to give it a miss;

3 you accept that skipping some bits may affect your ability to successfully get as much out of some of the later activities as you might have otherwise got.

As you work your way through the book try to be non-defensive and utterly realistic with yourself, after all you're not submitting answers to be marked by someone else, this is truly a self-actualisation activity!

Be reflective. Reflective in several ways:

a) You should try to see yourself as others see you.

b) You should try to view your actions and behaviour as others will view them.

c) You should be intellectually reflective and think carefully about the exercises you undertake with this book.

d) You need to be intellectually reflective about the career decisions you make, both in the long and short terms.

e) You should be prepared to look into the rear-view mirror of your life and learn from *your* past, be it last week or 20 years ago.

f) Act as a mirror to other people's experiences; don't just copy them exactly, but turn them to your view and see if you can learn from their experiences.

As you read through this book you will notice that there are some quotations from famous people – Churchill, Colin Powell, Eleanor Roosevelt and similar. There are also several quotes from 'real' people, people I meet or interact with on a daily basis, people with real, ordinary everyday careers sharing their wisdom.

CHAPTER 1

Your life goals and your legacy

Hang on a minute, this book is supposed to be about careers, not life goals! But let's just take stock for a moment:

- On average you will spend around 40 hours at work from Monday to Friday. Most of us work for 45 years . . . that is roughly 86,400 hours out of 292,000 . . . or around 30 per cent of your time, assuming that you live to 70.

- Your career is going to heavily influence where you live, whom you marry, how long you stay married, how many children you can afford to have, the quality of the material things you have during your working life and the comfort of your retirement.

- Even if you are born to a career, you still have choices about how that career will run and how you will behave during it. Most people would agree that Elizabeth Windsor has some fairly strong and challenging career goals that relate to leaving the monarchy stronger than she inherited it, even though she never had much choice about the career she would pursue.

Before we embark on the detail of career planning, it is actually quite important to consider some of the bigger philosophical questions that may either:

a) form the foundation of much of your future thinking and behaviour; or

b) suddenly cause you to ask yourself at some stage in the future, what the heck you are doing with your life.

You live in a free world and therefore you have a high degree of influence over your future career. Yes, your principles will have to be soluble in money to the point that every human being needs to eat, but this still gives you the right and the responsibility to make choices based on your overall opinion of why you are on this planet.

Let's take the example of someone with a strong Christian faith as the bedrock of their existence. They may then decide on any one of the following goals, goals that, on the surface, are pretty similar, but the implication of changing a few words can be profound:

A life goal 'to *glorify* God' could lead them to becoming a nun or a monk and spending a large part of their day in prayer.

If their life goal is 'to do God's *work*', they may find the life of prayer inadequate and so become a teaching or nursing nun or monk, a missionary or a priest.

Whereas someone with a life goal '*to live according to God's word*' will open themselves up to a wider selection of careers, but they will choose one that doesn't conflict with their overall principles.

Someone who has no particular religion or faith may take a humanist approach with similarly varying levels of commitment:

I wish to dedicate my life to helping others.

I wish to live without harming others.

I wish to take no responsibility for others, but to simply have a clear conscience.

Note that all the above goals are *infinite* . . . it doesn't matter how long you live, or what you actually achieve. They are also completely individual, it doesn't matter what is going on around you in the wider world, you can still glorify God, do God's work or live according to God's word. Similarly, you can still dedicate your life to helping others, or living without harming others.

On the other hand, setting a life goal that is *finite*, can be limiting in one way or another. For example, if you set a life goal 'to find a cure for cancer', there are two possible scenarios:

1 What do you do when a cure for cancer is found?

2 Will your life have been a failure if cancer is not cured by the time you reach retirement age?

I'm not saying this aspiration is wrong! You simply have to be aware that an achievable goal with a tangible end is a very laudable objective for a period of your life, but it may leave you at a loss if it is your life goal and you complete it before the end of your life, or if you don't!

Similarly, setting a life goal that relies heavily on factors *outside your control* is also fraught with problems. Suppose you set out your life goal 'to eradicate poverty'. And you even set limits that relate to a specific geographical area. Once you eradicate poverty in *that* area, the area suddenly becomes very attractive to the poor of *other areas*. They migrate in and, hey presto, your goal is undone.

When I was young and free and my imagination had no
*   limits,*
I dreamed of changing the world.
As I grew older and wiser I discovered the world would
*   not change*
So I shortened my sights somewhat and decided to
*   change only my country,*
But it too seemed immovable.
As I grew into my twilight years,
In one last desperate attempt,
I settled for only changing my family, those closest to me,
But alas, they would have none of it.
And now I realise as I lie on my deathbed,
If I had only changed myself first,
Then by example I might have changed my family,
From their inspiration and encouragement
I would then have been able to better my country,
And who knows, I might have changed the world.
FROM A TOMB IN WESTMINSTER ABBEY

For some of us a life goal may be something to which we have never given any thought; indeed, for some people the very concept of thinking about 'life, the universe and everything' gives us a headache. But if you have recently had a life-changing experience, you may already have started thinking about what it is all about.

In Chapter 8 we'll look at the issue of future-proofing your career and the way that most people find that their life goals change and evolve as they grow up and grow older and (theoretically) wiser. Don't worry about that while you are covering this chapter; just address your current situation. Avoid getting too bogged down in considering the fact that you may have had a plan and it has either led you down the wrong path or been sent awry . . . make a fresh start by asking the following searching philosophical questions.

WHY AM I HERE?

If you have a religious background, of virtually any type, then this question may be fairly simple to answer. However, it is worth just reassessing your answer: think about whether it is truly *your* answer or, when you give it some thought, is it actually the answer you were provided with by your parents, teachers or community when you were too young to reach your own conclusions?

Without taking too much time over this particular subject, it is worth remembering that the ability to ask this question is sometimes cited as what sets humans apart from other animals . . . we can question rather than simply act from instinct.

> *Why it's worth it: Having your own understanding of why you exist is one of the single most important ways to avoid just suffering 'the slings and arrows of outrageous fortune'. It forms the basis of your right to make your own decisions about life rather than seeing your destiny as pre-ordained.*

WHAT DO I WANT TO BE KNOWN FOR?

Stephen Covey developed *The 7 Habits of Highly Effective People*, a book I urge you to read if you haven't already done so. One of the habits is 'Begin with the end in mind'. So, imagine that you are a ghost at your funeral and describe the scene:

- Is the place packed or empty, intimate or highly managed?
- Is the press there? If so, why? Are you loved and famous or notorious?
- Are people mourning you or celebrating your life?
- Are the seats for family full of younger people or virtually empty?
- Are you encased in gold, oak, wicker, plywood or cardboard? Why? Was it your choice or to spite you?
- Imagine a eulogy made by a close family member; it could be your spouse/partner or your immediate issue, a son or daughter.

- First question is, is there anyone close to you who would actually want to say anything? Does anybody care?

- Assuming someone does, how would this person look? Financially successful or poor?

- How does this person act? Confident or terrified of speaking in public?

- What do they say about you and your life? Is it all true? Is any of it a surprise to the assembled people? Are they proud of you and your life or slightly ashamed? Do *they* actually care?

Write out the eulogy you hope would be made by this family member. It doesn't have to be autobiographical in length – Earl Spencer gave a eulogy for the Princess of Wales that is only 1,206 words but many feel that it is a most powerful evocation of her life.

- Imagine the eulogy given by a 'work' acquaintance; this could be a boss or a co-worker, an employee, a client or a supplier.

- Again the first question is, does anybody actually care enough about you to speak in public?

- What does this person look like? Prosperous or down-at-heel?

- How do they act? Proud to speak about you or indifferent? Or pleased that you are gone!

- What do they say about you? And what do they really mean? Were you a 'pleasure' to work with or . . . ?

Write out the eulogy you hope would be made by this work associate, again it doesn't have to be a tome; Winston Churchill's eulogy for Franklin D. Roosevelt was only 1,851 words.

"They say such nice things about people at their funerals that it makes me sad that I'm going to miss mine by just a few days." GARRISON KEILLOR, AUTHOR AND HUMORIST.

- Finally, if there was a gravestone, mausoleum or a plaque in the Garden of Remembrance or on the church wall, what would be the inscription your next of kin chose?

There is no right or wrong answer to any of the questions above, and there are no better or worse answers either. But the answers that you give for yourself will tell you much about your overall goals in life, and if your answers were virtually all 'I don't know' or even 'I don't care', then you might want to take a bit more time to think about the questions.

> *Why it's worth it: Think about it . . . your funeral is the final word on your life; by looking at the aspects in the activity, you cover everything from the ethical to the financial, from the family to the work, to the balance between the two.*

CASE STUDY

In 1965 the 20-year-old Pete Townsend wrote the lyric 'I hope I die before I get old' for The Who's legendary anthem *My Generation*. His band mate, Keith Moon, achieved this life goal but Townsend didn't. He is now a late-sixty-something millionaire and rock legend . . . not a bad place to be . . . but did he ever *really* hope he'd die before he got old?

Source: www.CartoonStock.com

WHAT DO I WANT TO BE REMEMBERED FOR?

The last days of Tony Blair's premiership (and the first days of the rest of his life) were dominated in the media by the issue of 'his legacy' – how would history judge him? What would he be remembered for? It later emerged that he had cared about this for some years before his departure from No. 10 ever became imminent.

You may not aspire to be a prime minister, president, or even to be famous, but you will still leave a legacy after you are gone.

Look first at the legacy you wish to leave 'immediately'. For several generations it has been an almost universal objective for humans to leave the next generation 'better off' than their own. This isn't just a matter of 'social climbing'. Governments have generally striven to upgrade the standard of living of the population, as well as each person wanting to leave their children with a better start in life than they had.

Traditionally, this has been measured predominantly in financial terms, though management speaker Chris Widener recommends a more holistic approach. The next activity is based on his 'seven point plan':

Emotional legacy

This relates to how you treat other people and how that affects them emotionally. Are you simply treating people the way you have been treated, or are you treating them in a way that you think is beneficial for them and is the way you want to be remembered?

- Are you raising your children in a way that will help them to be both independent and interdependent, or is your approach to them likely to affect them in negative ways?

- Are you helping your spouse or partner to grow emotionally?

- How about your parents? (It is worth bearing in mind that, as life expectancy increases, your children will probably treat you in your dotage in the same way that you treat your parents in theirs!)

How will you be remembered? As an abusive parent or as a wonderful parent? As a grateful and loving child or as a thankless offspring? As a supportive spouse or a restrictive influence?

Spiritual/ethical legacy

Widener calls this the 'god' question. Many people take the view that their offspring can be left to 'figure it out on their own'; and while in direct respect to 'god' this may be a sound approach, most of the world's legal systems are based on religious teachings somewhere down the line (even secular nations' laws are based on something similar to the 10 commandments.)

Are you helping and encouraging those around you to find their ethical/spiritual life? This may seem woolly, but consider recent scandals where the alleged culprit, clearly seen to be 'wrong' in the eyes of all, has fallen back on the defence of 'I didn't break any rules'. It may keep them out of jail but their legacy is tainted for ever.

Are you setting the kind of example that you want your offspring to emulate? Do they know what your ethical yardsticks are? Are you sufficiently consistent for them to know what you would do in a tricky situation?

Physical and health legacy

Are you leaving a legacy of health for your immediate family? No, you cannot prevent passing on your genes, warts and all, but what about your bad habits?

Eating, smoking, exercise and drinking are perhaps the most obvious, but what about your other health-related habits? Do you wear your seatbelt and drive safely? Do you rewire the house without turning off the electricity? Do you work ridiculously long hours? Do you take work on holiday (do you take holiday)?

> *Are you setting an example that your children will follow? Will you be proud if they do?*

Financial legacy

This is a two-parter:

1 Are you passing on a tangible financial legacy of assets?
2 Are you passing on a legacy of financial prudence and sense to your children?

Read it and reap activities

If you are not financially astute at present it is never too early or late to change this. The two books below will form the bedrock of this knowledge:

The Wealthy Barber, by David Chilton, 1997, Three Rivers Press.

This book will help you achieve the first part of your financial legacy.

Rich Dad Poor Dad: What the rich teach their kids about money that the poor and middle class do not!, by Robert T. Kiyosaki, 2011, Plata Publishing.

And this classic book will make you think about the way your attitude to money may be passed onto those around you and form your intangible legacy.

While you read these books, reflect on what you learn from them. When you have finished, take a short while to consider and then write down the five main things that you have gained from the read. Which of these elements would you deem worthy of passing on to others? Write a brief 'review' of the book. If you want to, post this on a website such as **amazon.com** or a book club review site.

Intellectual legacy

What are you doing that challenges your sphere of influence to intellectual gain? And are you encouraging this in your family? Do you read ''improving texts' or are you stuck in the chick lit and thriller genres? Do you read books or are you strictly a magazine reader? What are your television viewing habits – soaps and reality television, or documentaries and current affairs?

> *Will those left after you are gone say that you made them think thoughts they hadn't before? Would you want them to? Did you challenge them to be smarter/better read/more informed?*

Now let's look at the longer-term legacy; not those who actually know you but your descendants three or four generations in the future. In the UK and the USA in the early years of the twenty-first century there was an increasing and widespread interest in genealogy and family history. Celebrities queued up to appear on television programmes such as *Who Do You Think You Are?*, and over five million people (in the UK version alone) regularly watched actors and other famous people uncovering their ancestors' legacies. Interestingly, some of them had a good understanding of their family tree and the lives and loves of their forebears, while in other cases some of them discovered skeletons in the closet that, had they known about them before the cameras arrived, would probably have motivated them to turn down their agent's advances.

How do you want history to judge you? Imagine your great-great-granddaughter asking her mum about you:

- Will her mother actually know anything? If she knew nothing, would that hurt you?
- What would you want her to be aware of or find out about your life?

■ What would you be ashamed to have discovered about your career? Or your private life?

■ Would you hope that the family already knew some/much/all about you?

■ Would you want them to know that your life formed a foundation for their financial situation? If so, what foundation . . . poverty or wealth?

■ Would you want them to be able to travel to see a statue/blue plaque of you . . .

■ . . . or something that you had been responsible for, such as a painting in a museum, a book in a library or a building/road/bridge?

■ Do you want your name to be synonymous with a physical object, such as the Hoover . . . or the Kalashnikov?

■ Or synonymous with an action or behaviour?

> . . . Luddite
>
> Noun – an opponent of industrial change or innovation. [C19: alleged to be named after Ned Ludd, an eighteenth-century Leicestershire workman, who destroyed industrial machinery.]
>
> . . . or Draconian
>
> Adjective – disproportionate severity; derives from Draco, an Athenian justice under whom small offences carried heavy punishments.
>
> . . . or Churchillian
>
> Adjective – suggestive of Winston Churchill, e.g. defiant, witty, indomitable.

. . . or Einstein

> Noun – possessive of a monstrous intellect, as in 'Oh
> he's a real Einstein, he got a first from Cambridge, you
> know', or 'You don't have to be an Einstein to see
> that . . .'.

THE LAST WORDS ABOUT YOUR LIFE GOALS

If you have ever seen the film *The Bucket List* you'll know
what a bucket list is: it is a list of things that you want to do
before you die. In the film the two characters are motivated
by the fact that they are both terminally ill, but that shouldn't
be the only reason to have a bucket list. Make up your
bucket list of things you want to do before major milestones
in your life:

- things to do before I settle with a partner;
- things to do before I become a parent;
- things to do before 50;
- things to do before retirement;
- things to do before I die.

Not only will this help to give you something to concentrate
on, rather than whiling away your life in the pub or in front of
the television, but it will also save you from getting to these
milestones and thinking 'I wish I'd . . .'.

It will also give you a bit of a head start on some of the later
activities in this book!

CHAPTER 2

Your values and beliefs

WHAT ARE MY VALUES?

We all have values – principles that guide our thought processes, our judgements, our decisions and our behaviours. Sometimes we see people labelled as 'unprincipled', but this really just means that the person has principles that are different from those of others, specifically the local majority.

Our values come from a range of sources:

Our parents; their values by osmosis	Our reaction to early experiences at the hands of parents, guardians, teachers and playmates
Our schooling: primary and secondary	Our friends' values
The society in which we are raised	The media we are exposed to as youngsters
The religious or political atmosphere of our culture	

We generally develop deep-seated values at an early age; indeed the Jesuit education system used to say:

> *Give me the boy to the age of seven and I will give you back the man.*

But our values are not set in stone. As we develop into adulthood we start to create our own self-chosen values; this is often seen as the 'rebellious' stage in teenagers, when they sometimes take an oppositional stance to the values that they feel were imposed on them as youths. Virtually all generations have undergone this stage, it is not a modern phenomenon. It just seems that way because in the twenty-first century the communication media give rebellious youth more of a voice than it ever had before!

Our values will not only be moulded by our spirit of independence but also by various other factors:

1 Our burgeoning capacity to see through the (perhaps well-meaning) fibs of our parents, teachers and religious leaders. For example, we come to realise that life is not as 'fair' as our teachers led us to believe it should be; there ARE winners and losers in life. Father Christmas does not exist and being good isn't a guarantee of reward. Oh, and our elders are not necessarily our betters.

> *Rule 1: 'Life is not fair – get used to it'. Erroneously attributed to Bill Gates, Kurt Vonnegut and Brooks Coleman in a speech allegedly containing 10 (or 13) rules for students embarking on a career. Actually drawn from Charles J. Sykes' book* Dumbing Down Our Kids.

2 Our experiences at the hands of friends, lovers, employers and co-workers. The naivety of youth gives way to the cynicism of the battered.

3 Our wider reading of the media. Whereas we may have been brought up in a home that only took one newspaper with one particular editorial slant, as we get older we may read others or choose to watch a wider range of current affairs programmes on television.

4 The results of our own actions and inactions. As we grow up, we 'test the boundaries' of acceptable behaviour; the reactions of others (or their total lack of reaction) allows us to form our own values.

5 Our continued or renewed trust in the authority figures of our childhood. Witness radicalisation of adolescents to extreme views by others whom they perceive as priests, imams or prophets.

Regardless of what our values are, they are behind every decision we make. People with strongly held values, whether they be deemed extreme or not, tend to exhibit those values in all their decisions, behaviours and actions:

- Germans in the 1930s who valued Aryan supremacy and a belief in the evil of the Jewish faith tended to become Nazi persecutors;

- people who believe in the sanctity of human life tend to actively support anti-abortion groups;

- people who believe that their god will reward them for martyrdom often follow the jihad;

- and people who value animal life and health often become veterinarians.

You regularly see companies and organisations publicly declaring their values on their websites, in their advertising or even in their 'mission statements'. Often these have been generated by groups of employees deliberately identifying the values they wish to work with day to day and to be judged by, both by customers and in their annual appraisals.

Below is a list of personality traits. It isn't exhaustive, but it aims to give you a really good start at identifying your attitudes and thought processes. Look at each term and ask yourself if it is an attribute that you, personally, at this stage of your life, hold to be *important*. If it is, highlight it. It doesn't matter whether it is a characteristic that you display *at present*, you must think of your inner dialogue and your personal motivators.

Adaptability	Appreciativeness	Audaciousness
Adventurousness	Approachability	Benevolence
Aggressiveness	Assertiveness	Boldness
Altruism	Assuredness	Bravery
Ambition	Attentiveness	Buoyancy

Calmness	Efficiency	Indiscretion
Carefulness	Egocentricity	Ingenuity
Charitableness	Empathy	Inquisitiveness
Charm	Encouragement	Insightfulness
Cheerfulness	Energy	Inspired nature
Commitment	Entertaining nature	Inspiratory
Compassion	Enthusiasm	Intelligence
Confidence	Expressiveness	Intensity
Conformity	Extravagance	Introversion
Consistency	Extroversion	Intuitiveness
Contentedness	Fairness	Inventiveness
Conviviality	Faithfulness	Judiciousness
Cooperativeness	Flexibility	Judgement
Courageousness	Focus	Justness
Courteousness	Frankness	Kindness
Creativity	Friendliness	Learning
Curiosity	Fun	Liberality
Decisiveness	Gallantry	Logic
Decorousness	Generosity	Loyalty
Deference	Gentility	Meekness
Dependability	Giving nature	Meticulousness
Determination	Gregariousness	Modesty
Devotedness	Helpfulness	Obedience
Dignity	Heroism	Open-mindedness
Diligence	Honesty	Optimism
Discipline	Honour	Originality
Discretion	Hopefulness	Outlandishness
Dominance	Hospitality	Passion
Dutifulness	Humility	Peace
Dynamism	Humour	Perfectionism
Eagerness	Impartiality	Persistence
Effectiveness	Independence	Persuasiveness

Philanthropy	Sensitivity	Tranquillity
Practicality	Servility	Trustingness
Privacy	Shrewdness	Trustworthiness
Punctuality	Sincerity	Unflappability
Realism	Skilfulness	Unifying nature
Reasonableness	Solitariness	Uniqueness
Refinement	Spontaneity	Usefulness
Reliability	Stability	Vigorousness
Resilience	Supportiveness	Virtuousness
Respectability	Thankfulness	Visionariness
Respectfulness	Thoroughness	Vivacity
Selfishness	Thoughtfulness	Warmth
Selflessness	Thrift	
Self-obsession	Tidiness	
Self-reliance	Traditionalism	

Once you have highlighted the traits that you hold to be important to you, group them in affinity areas – in other words the ones that 'go together'. For instance:

1 benevolence, charitableness, compassion, faithfulness, generosity, a giving nature and hospitality might go together;

2 adventurousness, boldness, energy, outlandishness and self-reliance might go together;

3 confidence, creativity, egocentricity, an entertaining nature, extroversion, fun, inspiratory and inventiveness might go together.

Write these out in their groups.

Now that you have grouped the chosen words together, study each group and test the decision; are these really characteristics that either:

a) describe your behaviours and attitudes genuinely; or

b) describe your inner thoughts?

Rather than the characteristics that you think other people (your parents, friends, colleagues or family) would *want* you to display.

Remove or amend any that aren't *your real* values.

Once you have decided which are indeed your own genuine current or desired attributes, the next thing to do is to find a way of encapsulating each group into one simple value statement. For example, you might want to sum up group 1 as:

> *I am a benevolent person; my actions are guided by a commitment to compassion and generosity in all things to the best of my ability.*

Write these down.

There is no real right or wrong outcome for this; so long as you clearly know what you mean. Likewise, there is no minimum or maximum number of value statements you can or should have . . . for some people one or two is more than adequate, others feel more comfortable having several. The important factor is to deliberately consider what your values are before they are put to the test.

Consider whether these values are the same as the ones you might have held five years ago and reflect on whether they are the same as when:

- you left school/college/university;
- you left home;
- you got married/involved with your (first and subsequent) partner(s);
- you became a parent;
- you first lost a job.

Consider whether these values are likely to remain unchanged in the future if:

- you lose your income;
- you lose your partner;
- you lose your parent(s);
- you lose a child;
- you (or your parent, child, partner) fall(s) seriously ill.

WHAT IS THE COMPARATIVE LEVEL OF IMPORTANCE OF EACH?

Next, it is valuable to try to rank your values in a relative order of their importance to you; perhaps the best way to do this is a paired comparison.

Compare each value against the other values one by one, and ask which is the more important of the two. So, for instance, my values are titled as:

A Benevolence

B Adventurousness

C Traditionalism

D Meticulousness

E Inventiveness

Comparing each to each other:

Value	A	B	C	D	E
A					
B	B				
C	A	B			
D	A	B	C		
E	E	B	E	E	

(The grid above is simply a way to show that in the comparison between A and B, B is deemed more important, between A and C, A is more important and so on.)

Finally, tot up the number of times each value comes out top to see a rated order of priority of your values. In this case:

A	Benevolence	2 points
B	Adventurousness	4 points
C	Traditionalism	1 point
D	Meticulousness	0 points
E	Inventiveness	3 points

So in priority order:

1 Adventurousness

2 Inventiveness

3 Benevolence

4 Traditionalism

5 Meticulousness

Now carry out a bit of hypothetical scenario planning.

WHAT WOULD YOU DO IF . . . ?

a) You went for a solitary walk in the country and found a brown envelope with a wad of used banknotes in it, about four months' income?

b) You discovered at work that one of your senior managers was fiddling the books and diverting significant quantities of money and/or material for their own personal benefit?

c) A friend invited you to join them in an illegal scam that could net you a lot of money with very little risk of being caught?

d) When driving home on a dark, rainy night you saw a person trudging along the road, soaked to the skin and in obvious distress?

e) You received a telephone call at work from a head-hunter who invited you to apply for a lucrative job with your current major competitor.

f) After work you were having a drink with a close friend who suddenly told you about the passionate affair they have been having behind their spouse's back for the last three months?

g) The friend in f) above asked you to lie to their spouse about a team-building event so they could slip off with their lover for a 'dirty weekend'?

h) Your sibling developed a medical condition that required a bone marrow transplant but it had to be done at a time that would leave you sick in hospital right through the most important stage in your career?

j)   You won the Lottery . . . 620 times your annual salary?

h)   After the death of the last of your parents you went to the reading of the will to be told that the will was changed in the last month to leave everything to your sibling?

There is no right or wrong answer to these scenarios and you don't have to discuss them with anyone else; the objective is to self-test your own reactions, which will be based on your real values.

Once you have considered each of these scenarios and decided on your reaction, look back at your list of values and check whether your likely behaviours match your aspirational values. This is a good way to test whether you were being realistic, without exposing yourself to any real danger!

USING YOUR VALUES TO HELP YOU CHOOSE A CAREER

Your values won't tell you what job you should be applying for, or what career you should be entering or changing to, but they will help you to define the type of role that you may find either enjoyable and successful or distasteful and difficult. They may also help you to define the type of organisation that you might find matches your values and therefore is fertile ground for your career.

Consider the types of values you have identified within yourself. You will find that some of these naturally point you towards certain types of career. For instance, if you have identified that you typify 'confidence, creativity, egocentricity, an entertaining nature, extroversion, fun, inspiratory and inventiveness' then a career in advertising or the creative arts may seem the sort of career that is aligned to your values. Whereas the same list of values may encourage you away from a career in accountancy or finance, regardless of anyone else's expectations, or the money.

However, you need to look at things holistically and if, as well as the values above, you also value 'dignity, consistency, peace, reliability and tranquillity' then a career in the performing arts may not be appropriate. At this stage you may start to consider a career that pays the bills and an extracurricular life that fulfils your higher needs. See Chapter 3 for more information regarding motivation.

Look at the websites of different organisations and make a note of the mission statements and values they publish. Read between the lines as well. Virtually every organisation in the world will say that it 'focuses on its customers' and it 'recognises the value of its staff', so look a bit deeper to see what type of customers they have/what levels of satisfaction they achieve, how many people they employ and what their staff turnover rates are.

Start scanning the recruitment advertisements and organisations' website pages headed 'Careers', 'Opportunities', 'Vacancies' or 'Working with us'. Look for the characteristics they say are essential and those that would be desirable. Again, be aware that job adverts seldom tell the whole truth; they tend to gloss over the boring bits and make every job sound as if it were absolutely critical and utterly fascinating. What you will often find is that the values the organisation is seeking are articulated in the job advert or the job specification, either explicitly or implicitly.

As an example, see the table on the opposite page.

No matter how good a job looks on paper, look also at the values you hold that just don't appear at all; for example in the case opposite, independence, liberality, fun, vivacity, adventurousness, audaciousness. If these are values you hold but they just don't feature at all in the job specification, then once the initial novelty wears off you may find that the job bores you to death.

The job advertisement	The values required:
The role is required to provide Risk/Issues management into the various projects being undertaken to *minimise risk of failure*(1) from Transition into a business-as-usual mode by providing specific focus on this critical period of contract development.	1) Diligence, Meticulousness
Develop(2) and *implement*(3) appropriate processes for management of Risk and Issues required for successful programme/transition delivery.	2) Ingenuity, Intelligence
	3) Discipline, Efficiency
Facilitate regular Risk & Issue reviews(4) ensuring that mitigation activities are identified, planned and managed.	4) Frankness, Perfectionism, Approachability
Provide Risk and Issues reports and highlight(5) any major areas of concern that may impact upon our ability to successfully deliver the Transition/Programme.	5) Commitment, Decisiveness, Diligence
Instigate Gate Reviews ensuring that *best practice*(6) is adhered to and that resulting actions are *completed*(7).	6) Traditionalism, Conformity
Liaise(8) with the Programme Director and project managers to ensure risks and issues are managed.	7) Effectiveness, Judiciousness
Undertake Lessons Learned *workshops*(9) to improve Transition and programme efficiency across business.	8) Gregariousness, Respectfulness
Document preparation(10) for meetings and assist with collation of management reports where necessary.	9) Learning, Inquisitiveness, Logic
Package on offer:	10) Consistency, Efficiency Punctuality
37 hours per week	11) Stability, Traditionalism, Consistency
Monday–Friday (11)	
25 days holiday	
Pension	
Healthcare	
Life assurance	

CHAPTER 3

Your likes and dislikes

"Setting career goals doesn't work for everyone, just make sure you know what you like (and dislike), what you are good at and whether enjoying a job is more important than promotion. Then be ready to seize opportunities as they arise." GRAHAM O'CONNELL, HEAD OF LEARNING & DEVELOPMENT STRATEGY AND CURRICULUM, CIVIL SERVICE

Work is a four-letter word. Historically work is seen as something that you *have* to do, indeed it has been called the curse of the working classes. You simply aren't supposed to enjoy it.

The common perception has been that the majority of us work to fulfil our *needs*; what Maslow and Hertzberg referred to as the Basic Motivators or the Hygiene Factors – food, water, shelter, security and safety. Certainly these are very important; it isn't easy to enjoy life when you are starving to death or homeless.

However, if you could find a career that not only provided you with the basic needs in life but also gave you real pleasure, then you would have hit on Nirvana, or as an old school friend, Jim Graham, put it: 'The secret of life is to find someone to pay you to do that which you would otherwise pay to do.'

I am one of those people who is happy to strike up a conversation with anyone at any time, and in mid 2011 I had an hour-long chat with a lady on a train at the end of a day's work in London. The lady was a lecturer in a further education college and she told me how she at first had been shocked to discover that a small but significant number of the female students had set their career goal on becoming WAGS (Wives And Girlfriends) of professional footballers.

Her initial shock had turned to distaste when she saw the clinical way the students had planned a detailed and concerted campaign of identifying suitable prospective husbands among the target 'market', categorising by:

- looks;
- style;
- current career position and reported earnings;
- competition (in terms of present girlfriend/wife);
- future earning power as a professional footballer (including likely location of owning club);
- past history of fidelity;
- long-term likely earning power: is he capable of going on to managerial positions when the active game is beyond him, or is he sufficiently articulate to land a role as a media soccer pundit, or sufficiently 'eye candy' to land lucrative product endorsement deals?

She was further surprised to witness the calculating way the students then networked among themselves to find ways to get into the hunting ground; finding out which nightclubs, restaurants, spas and hotels specifically targeted men frequented and precisely when were they there. Text messages arrived and girls leapt into action like fire-fighters to be on scene to effect an apparently casual or happenstance bumping-in-to.

Then my informant started to realise that, rather than being shocked or repulsed by this behaviour, secretly she actually felt a degree of admiration. The girls concerned were demonstrating a sound business approach to their careers based on their likes (wealth, celebrity and material possessions) and their values (Ego, Fun, Extroversion, Practicality, Self-obsession, Stability).

No laws were being broken, no footballers were being forced into marriages, pre-nuptial agreements were acceptable and the old adage that 'while you shouldn't marry for money, it does no harm to marry where money is' was being taken into account.

"WHY DID YOU THINK THE LAWYER GAVE ME SUCH A GOOD DEAL?"

Source: T. McCracken, www.mchumor.com

The girls had clearly divided the matter of their career choice into two distinct areas of 'likes':

a) the things they were happy to 'do' within this career, and

b) the outcomes that they wanted to 'get' as a result.

In this instance, the former is clearly to be the 'wife' of a footballer, and I don't think it necessary to detail what the role of a wife (or husband/partner) may entail. The latter is the lifestyle, material possessions, fame, security and opportunities that come as a consequence.

In order to obtain the material things in life you probably need to earn the money by the 'sweat of your brow'. In December 2011, the UK Channel 5 show *The Wright Stuff* ran a story relating to a family in which a woman was demanding that her husband give up his job and retrain as a lawyer in order that they should be able to afford to send their children to fee-paying schools. She was looking solely at the outcome of her husband's career rather than the work he would actually be doing on a day-to-day basis.

Would it make him *happy* to be a lawyer for 40 hours a week for the rest of his working life? Would he be prepared to sacrifice his day-to-day happiness (and sanity) in return for the belief that he was giving his children a better start in life? (We won't get into a values-based discussion relating to the rights and wrongs of fee-paying schools, the rights and wrongs of lawyers, or the fact that it was the wife who was demanding he change career, not him.)

ASSESSING YOUR LIKES AND DISLIKES

This sounds as if it is the easiest thing in the world, and frankly it isn't hard, but it is necessary to *differentiate* between your likes of the day-to-day activity of your career and your likes of the outcomes of your career.

These will fall into three categories: material likes, status likes and intangibles.

Material likes

Falling into both the day-to-day and the outcomes, material likes are the obvious tangible things that you enjoy about your career. They range from:

- the clothes you like to wear as part of your career 'uniform' (in the original TV series *Minder*, Arthur Daley used to refer to a desire to get into 'serious tie-wearing activities', whereas other people may baulk at the very idea of becoming a 'suit'.)

  . . . through to:

- the car you want to be entitled to/would like to be able to afford to buy as a result of your career position (this could range from being a test driver for Aston Martin because you love the cars, to being successful enough to buy and own a Rolls Royce);

- the benefits package that you want, which will range from the 'today' benefits such as healthcare, right through to the long-term benefits such as pension arrangements (even if you don't anticipate leaving this role aged sixty-something with a gold watch!).

Status likes

This area may link very clearly to your values. Status likes range from:

- the job title you want to have (do you want to be a secretary or a permanent secretary, a vice president of marketing or a bank manager, or a blacksmith?)

    . . . to the

- standing your position gives you in the community. In the operetta *The Pirates of Penzance* one of the characters declares 'Remember I'm a VIP, not the man from the Prudential'. Note that standing is not just about being a pillar of the establishment or being well paid; the pride you may get from being in uniform if you are a fire-fighter or the enjoyment of having a job that is very different to other people's are all status elements.

The intangibles

These cover a wide range; for instance:

- Your work location; do you want to be in one place or do you enjoy moving around? If you move around are you happy to move daily, weekly, monthly, with the seasons? Will this necessitate living close to where you are working and therefore having no everyday 'home'? If so, are you happy to be accommodated in a caravan, a B&B, a budget motel or a swanky five-star establishment with a spa and a top chef? Some people just love living in hotels and others hate it.

- Your work environment; do you want to be working in an office, a factory, out-of-doors or down a sewer? Do you prefer an environment that is frenetic and noisy or quiet and peaceful? Will YOU have any control over that? Do you prefer an environment that is clean and tidy or do you like an environment that means that you will leave work each day stinking of something?

- Your relationships with co-workers; do you want to have a boss on hand to ask advice from or would you rather be able to use your own initiative? Do you want to work as part of a team, relying on others and having mates to work with or would you be happier working alone?

- Your relationships with customers; do you want to see customers every day or are you happier never actually clapping eyes on them? Would you like to work in customers' homes or offices?

- The hours you want to work; do you prefer regular hours or shifts? Would you enjoy the variety of being on call or would you find it a terrible imposition? Do you want to work part time, now or in the future?

- Do you prefer a quiet environment or do you actively seek adventure? How much danger do you seek or are you prepared to accept? And how soluble is this in money? In the aftermath of the First Gulf War many young Sappers in the Royal Engineers were defusing mines and booby traps for a salary of about £30 a day . . . civilian contractors were doing the same work and getting paid several hundred pounds a day.

CASE STUDY

Steve was being made redundant from a large industrial establishment. As part of his job search he looked at his likes and dislikes and concluded that he liked working alone, he didn't like working in an office or building, he enjoyed the outdoors and preferred customers to colleagues, he wasn't fussed about other peoples' opinions of status, but he did like to be appreciated and to feel useful. He wasn't interested in earning big money but wanted a regular wage. He quite enjoyed being on call, so long as the other wants were fulfilled.

He found his perfect job! He works for Dyno-Rod: he has a little van and a mobile phone, he gets a call, goes to a householder's property, clears their blocked drains on his own, is always much thanked (and often tipped) and he gets paid at the end of every month.

In the modern world we are beginning to accept that the job you take today is unlikely to be the career you follow for the rest of your life, so you also need to consider some other intangible wants that relate to the future:

- What training or experience do you want to gain from the job you are looking for today?
- What contacts and market knowledge do you want to get from it?
- What reputation do you want to build based on this role?

(This aspect is looked at more in Chapter 8.)

LISTING YOUR LIKES

List all the things that you like and dislike. Use the headings below to help you cover all the bases.

A The actual day-to-day

   1 Likes

   2 Dislikes

B The outcomes

   1 Likes

   2 Dislikes

WHAT WOULD YOU DO IF . . .

Consider the following scenarios and answer for yourself as truthfully as you can.

1 How many hours a week would you be prepared to put in to the job to double your income?

2 How would you react if your employer wanted to relocate your job to another region/country, and asked you to relocate?

3 If you inherited enough money to pay off all your debts and have an unearned income equal to your current salary, what would you do?

4 What sort of day-to-day activities would you ask someone to delegate to you for the challenge and the enjoyment?

5 What sort of day-to-day activities would you gladly delegate or outsource if you could?

6 For how long would you be prepared to put your 'life' on hold in order to earn a large amount of money (see case studies below)?

CASE STUDIES

Many of the skilled workers in the oil and gas industry spend six months in the field, living on a rig, with only their workmates for company. They earn enough money to take the next six months off. Some pursue six months of pure hedonism while others pursue six months of family life after the separation. ('Absence makes the heart grow fonder.') Others pursue a recreation that may or may not bring a financial reward.

Many actors/musicians only get acting/playing jobs for short and irregular periods and these can be either very intensive (two, two-hour stage shows a day for seven days a week including travelling between venues) or require extensive travel (15 cities in a month on three different continents). These jobs can be adequately lucrative to allow them breathing space inbetween, or they may have a more 'ordinary' job to turn to in the interim.

Many professional sportsmen and women recognise that their chosen field is one where their working-life expectancy is very limited; for the most part, they will be past it by the time they are 25. They also practise 10–12 hours a day so have virtually no other life . . . but the lure of the glory, the huge salary, the sponsorship and endorsement deals and the future as a sports commentator are usually sufficient reward.

USING YOUR LIKES AND DISLIKES TO HELP YOU FIND THE 'RIGHT' CAREER

Up until now you have been thinking almost exclusively about yourself. Now you need to get out into the wide world and see what is going on outside your head.

A good place to start is to recognise that your intuitive knowledge of possible or probable career options is likely to be limited; so start by looking at wider listings of all careers rather than at the ones that come into your head. Listed below are some website addresses that have fairly wide listings; these are, of course, free to access.

http://www.careerplanner.com/ListOfCareers.cfm

http://www.bls.gov/k12/azlist.htm

http://jobsearch.about.com/od/jobsbycareerfieldlist/ Jobs_by_Career_Field_List.htm

Search the term 'career listings' and scroll down the lists looking at the titles. When you see one that sounds interesting take a further look at the entry, or use the title to search again until you find actual detail about the job itself.

For each potential career you consider, look at the two areas of day-to-day and outcomes in some detail. As an example we'll take a career as a police officer; the job description is drawn from **http://prospects.ac.uk/police_officer_job_ description.htm**.

First, let's look at the day-to-day role (solely for simplicity we'll use an example of an officer in London):

Day-to-day-activity	
Like	**Dislike**
Providing a visible presence to deter crime	Liaising with community groups and individuals
Conducting patrol duties on foot	Keeping the peace at public meetings, social events, processions, trade disputes or strikes
Developing community knowledge to identify individuals and locations at risk of being involved in crime	Acting with sensitivity when dealing with situations such as delivering news of a sudden death to a family or when dealing with sexual crimes
Responding to calls and requests from the public to assist at incidents	Taking statements and complying with relevant legal requirements
Diffusing potentially volatile situations with due regard to the safety of all involved	Preparing crime reports and presenting case files to senior officers and the Crown Prosecution Service (CPS)
Conducting initial investigations, gathering evidence	Completing administrative procedures

Like	Dislike
Interviewing suspects, victims and witnesses in accordance with relevant legislation	Submitting internal crime reports and criminal intelligence reports
Conducting arrests with due regard for the human rights, security and health and safety of detained individuals, members of the public, colleagues and self	Gathering, recording and analysing intelligence to achieve community safety and crime reduction objectives and providing crime prevention advice
Attending and giving evidence in court	Attending road-related incidents including collision scenes, vehicle checkpoints and traffic offences
Investigating and taking action on information received from members of the public	Enforcing road traffic legislation and issuing fixed penalties for relevant offences
	Dealing with lost or found property

As you can see in this example, the day-to-day role has a relatively even split of likes and dislikes, the latter being a combination of dull and boring, 'unsexy' and difficult (for me).

Now let's look at the outcomes of the job:

Outcomes	
Like	**Dislike**
Starting salary £22,680, rising to £25,617 on completion of initial training	Unsocial hours, shift work and emergency call-outs are a regular feature of the job
Typical salaries £35,610–£40,020 (Sergeant); £45,624–£49,488 (Inspector) £51,789–£53,919 (Chief Inspector)	The environment can at times be deeply harrowing
London weighting (up to £6,501) and additional payments are available for all	Police officers are expected to adhere to a dress code
Other benefits include free London travel, flexible working and key worker living benefits	Police officers are governed by a code of conduct both on and off duty
Police Pension Scheme provided	
The environment can be physically demanding and potentially dangerous	
The work is pressurised, with officers facing a continual succession of calls on their time and resources *Sometimes this is a 'like' (I enjoy pressure and a busy environment; it gives me a sense of achievement) and sometimes it is a 'dislike' (it is relentless and I can never unwind or relax)*	

Like	Dislike
Part-time working, job share and flexible hours are available; career breaks are possible after the probationary period	
Job opportunities exist throughout the UK and transfers between forces are possible dependent on position availability and the suitability of the officer concerned	

In this example the outcomes are more positive, with the dislikes being split between the 'dislike today', such as the dress code and code of conduct off duty, and the potential dislikes in the future, such as the possibility of becoming (di-) stressed and the anti-social hours becoming a problem in later life when married and a parent.

Having differentiated between the likes of the day-to-day and the likes of the outcomes, you need to decide on the comparative priorities: fundamentally this is a matter of 'How much of a sacrifice am I prepared to make in one for the sake of the other?' This may be in relation to work/life balance or it may be *within* an area. For example, you may be prepared to work varied shifts because the money makes it worthwhile, or it may be that you are prepared to work varied shifts because what you will actually be doing on the shifts is so enjoyable that you feel it is worth it. This may seem like a semantic quibble but it is important to recognise the differences. As time passes you may find the work loses its glamour and so you stay because the money is worthwhile . . . then if, comparatively, the financial reward starts to slip you suddenly realise that you are only doing the job because . . .?

IT AIN'T WHAT YOU KNOW IT'S WHO YOU KNOW

You can research the potential labour market as mentioned above using the internet and looking at job adverts and listings. You can also use networking.

Networking isn't about having hundreds of friends on Facebook, or about having influential schoolmates or relations who can pull strings (these things may well help but they are NOT prerequisites of successful networking).

The premise behind networking is linked to the concept of 'six degrees of separation'. Stanley Milgram first coined the term and the theory that we are all connected by no more than six different steps, and though his original work has since been questioned, more recent investigations by the BBC (anecdotal and not really scientific) and Microsoft (rather more statistical and analytical in nature) show that it is still the case that we can link to many other people who can offer a vast network of knowledge and connections, if we are just prepared to try.

Make a list of *all* the people you know – they don't have to be best friends or close relatives, and they don't have to be captains of industry or highly influential people, just people who you could reasonably have a five-minute conversation with, over the phone or face to face.

Basic principles

1 You are not asking them to give you a job.

2 You are not asking them to introduce you to someone whom you will ask to give you a job.

3 You are not going to ask them to lend or give you money (even though you may be unemployed and broke)!

4 You are not going to pour your heart out to them and ask for sympathy, they are not a therapist.

Now imagine having a conversation with them. You open by assuring them of the principles set out above and then you ask them about *their* experience of life and their contacts:

- What do/did they do?
- How did they get there?
- What made them go there?
- What do they enjoy about it?
- What was less fun?
- What were their workmates like?
- How did the industry work? Who supplied it? Who were the customers?
- Why are they still there? Or why did they leave?

Listen and ask further questions; this 'showing an interest' will generally make people relaxed and open about their past and their own experience.

Then share (briefly) what you are looking for and have to offer in terms of your values, your wants and your abilities, and link these back to their story, looking for similarities and connections.

Finally, ask if they can put you in touch with relevant people (perhaps ones they mentioned in the prior conversation) with whom you can have a similar discussion . . . reiterate if necessary that you are only trying to find out about options from the horse's mouth, not ask for a job.

You'll be amazed how helpful people can be with information, and you'll be amazed how rapidly you get to know about organisations and industries that you'd never previously heard of.

IF YOU CAN'T FIND AN OPENING IN A CAREER THAT YOU 'LIKE' . . .

If you cannot find a career that you like the sound of but you do have ideas of what you like (rather than having no idea at all) then you may be better off setting up your own business and employing yourself. Chapter 13 looks into this.

THE LAST WORDS ON LIKES AND DISLIKES

It is, and always has been, the case that if you like material possessions and you wish to have them in your life you have two options:

1 steal them;

2 buy them.

Which of these options you choose will depend on your values, but let us assume that you didn't steal this book and therefore propose to buy the material possessions and the lifestyle you want in life. To buy them you will need to earn money.

In *The Sound of Music* the character Maria Von Trapp sings of her favourite things: raindrops on roses, whiskers on kittens, bright copper kettles, warm woollen mittens and brown paper packages tied up with string. The band Big Brovaz sang of their favourite things: diamonds and rubies, Bentleys and Mercedes cabriolets and platinum rings.

The former is looking at the simpler things in life – they are free or cheap and therefore don't require hundreds of hours of effort to achieve them. Increasingly people are recognising the value of enjoyment of the less materialistic wants: less stress, less family pressure, fewer disappointments, probably lower levels of personal debt. You don't have to be a hippy living in a commune to eschew the traditional approach to 'ambition'.

Take a look back at the lists of likes that you have generated in the previous activities in this chapter and ask yourself one last time, 'Am I going to be happy working the necessary hours in the necessary places in order to earn the necessary money to fund the things I want in life?'

CHAPTER 4

Balancing your work and your life

According to the Center for American Progress, 90 per cent of working mothers and 95 per cent of working fathers report work–family conflict. But work/life balance isn't solely a topic for those with a family; single people are entitled to a work/life balance too – they may want to devote out-of-hours time to relaxing, exercising, socialising or doing community work.

The utopian view of the post-war years that increasing technology would give people more away-from-the-workplace quality time has proven largely wrong; technology binds many of the working population to the office while they are commuting, relaxing or even on holiday. Those who aren't in 'white collar' jobs are working longer hours as competition and globalisation bring new challenges to all walks of life.

The concept of work/life balance, though it has been around since the 1970s, is not universally accepted and is not one where there are absolute rights and wrongs. It's one where you need to understand what it means to you.

WHAT IS 'WORK/LIFE BALANCE'?

In order to define what work/life balance means to *you*, consider the following questions:

1 *What emotional response does the phrase 'work/life balance' trigger in you?*
Do you see it as a families-only policy for parents? Is it a human right? Is it a topic for employer policies? Who controls work/life balance? Is it a tool for militants to use to get more time off?

2 *How much do you love your present job?*
Does your work enthral and enervate you or bore you rigid?

3 *How much do you like the organisation you work for?*
Do you respect your boss and your boss's boss or do you think they are donkeys leading lions? How about your co-workers; are they great people to work with and play with, or a bunch of losers with whom you hate socialising?

4 *What is your opinion of the people who use the products and/or services you produce?*
Are they good people who you feel motivated to serve, do you not care about them at all, or do you see them as a pain in the proverbial?

5 *How do you feel about your job title?*
Are you proud of it or do you try to avoid mentioning it, or even tell people something else?

6 *What is the **real impact** of work/life balance and imbalance on you?*

Consider these questions carefully; the answers you give to yourself will give you a good understanding of not only the time element of the work/life balance but also the happiness element. We'll now look at each of these elements in turn.

The Time Element

Different people seek different things in their lives. This means that what would cripple one person is the very lifeblood of another.

CASE STUDY

A successful business executive was approaching her 60th birthday. She had amassed a not-inconsiderable fortune and was currently the Chief Executive of a multi-million-pound pharmaceutical company. Her husband, concerned about the long hours she still worked and her general health, asked her to start to downshift. She eventually agreed and informed the board of her intention to resign and move to a non-executive role as Chair.

Within a matter of days she started to receive phone calls offering her other non-executive roles. Within a matter of months she was working seven days a week and was blissfully happy. Her husband remained concerned!

And it is not just the financially successful . . .

CASE STUDY

Christian is a tree surgeon, it is a job he loves. His business is small – just himself and two young men in training. Christian inherited his home from his mother 23 years ago, has no loans or credit cards, small savings and a private pension fund that will provide for an adequate old age . . . if he ever starts drawing it. Christian is still working between three and five days a week climbing and felling trees at the age of 72, because he just loves doing it.

When considering the time element, ask yourself how much of your time (on a daily and whole-of-life basis) you will be happy allocating to your job as opposed to your other interests in life. This is not likely to be a constant for all people, not everyone actually wants eight hours' labour, eight hours' leisure and eight hours' rest. Nor will it be a constant for any one person. You might feel that at certain stages of your life you are happy to dedicate more hours to your work at the expense of your leisure time, whereas at other times in your life you may want or need to devote more hours to the 'leisure' activities of child-rearing or looking after elderly parents.

Things will also vary according to the work you do. Many teachers would consider themselves still to be 'at work' in the evening when they are running the school amateur dramatic club. And many self-employed people see their work as something they will gladly devote time to at 6 o'clock on a Sunday morning as well as all hours in the working week.

Inevitably, a large influence on the amount of time you are prepared to dedicate to being in work mode will depend on the level of reward and recognition you feel that you get from your work; if you feel unappreciated at work then you probably won't be happy spending 15 hours a day there, whereas if you feel that your boss and your customers respect and value you, you may be perfectly happy to work all hours.

Ask yourself:

How many hours in each day am I prepared to dedicate to work?

How many to travelling to and from work?

At what time of each day do I want or need to get away from work?

What is it that I intend to do in my 'leisure' time? Is it productive or restorative?

Are the answers above driven by my wants or the wants of other people?

How long will these requirements stay in place?

"I know quite a few people who work in Banking and Law etc. and earn 10 times what I do but also do 50 times more work including weekends . . . not my idea of a life!" STEVE ROBSON, SENIOR TECHNICAL TRAINING SPECIALIST, LLOYDS REGISTER.

The Happiness Element

In the land of the free there are three fundamental principles that were destined to guide the nation: the right to life, liberty and the pursuit of happiness. Happiness is a subjective thing:

- a sadist is happy inflicting pain;
- a masochist is happy having pain inflicted on them;
- many of us are made unhappy by either.

We have all heard of the poor little rich kid, or seen celebrities who appear to have everything, complaining about how tough their lives are and how depressed it makes them. On the flip side, life and literature are full of examples of people living in poverty and squalor who are happy with their lot. In Chapter 3 we looked at happiness in the context of likes and dislikes on a hypothetical basis. Now we are going to look at the reality of happiness.

Several of the activities in previous chapters have referred to elements of the work/life balance with regard to *planning* a career, but let's take a look at the situation for those who are in a career and may already be experiencing work/life conflict.

WORK/LIFE BALANCE ANALYSIS

1 Work

Using the format below consider the percentage of time that falls into each row. Be honest with yourself; don't exaggerate either way, consider the 'average' week. A week contains 168 hours.

Activity	Hours	Percentage
At work: these are the actual hours that you spend at your work (this may not be all working . . . it also includes the time you waste waiting for other people!)		
Preparing to work: the time it takes to prepare any work wear, pick out your clothes, get dressed and travel to *and from* work		
Psychologically winding-down: after work, changing from being a manager or employee to being a husband, wife, dad, mum or whatever		
Working out-of-hours: this includes reading up on work documents, doing work-related and employer-directed learning, taking work-related phone calls from colleagues or customers and so on; factor in any hours spent over the weekend or on holiday		
Total (just as a sanity check!)		

2 Life

Next consider, in the same way, the time you spend in out-of-work activities.

Activity	Hours	Percentage
Being a family member: spending quality time with your children/step-children/parents/siblings or relations		
Being a citizen: doing something unpaid in the community, regardless of whether it is as an elected councillor, a Special Constable, a volunteer labourer digging out the village pond or just taking a cup of tea with the widow next door		
Being at leisure: doing what you enjoy – it could be working out or Zumba, or it could be something solitary such as reading or walking or something social, like playing darts in the local		
Being a friend: helping out your mates, either by listening to their gripes or helping with a move, babysitting or fixing their tyre		
Being a spouse or partner: spending quality time with your significant other, being there for them, sharing their life and loves		

Being a congregant: not necessarily of a formal religious body but on a spiritual/ethical plain, following a football club, being a Guide leader or mentoring young offenders		
Being a student: learning something because *you* want to, this could be a language or a life skill or something self-generated but career relevant; it can be formal (adult education/correspondence course) or informal (reading, practising)		
Total (just as a sanity check; add these to the total in the previous table's columns and make sure that they add up to 168 and 100 per cent respectively!)		

Once you have totted up the totals, ask yourself

> *'Do I have a satisfactory balance between my working week and my life week?'*

There is no 'acceptable norm' it is a matter of personal acceptance; are *you* happy with it?

"Have fun in your command. Don't always run at a break-neck pace. Take leave when you've earned it." COLIN POWELL, US STATESMAN AND RETIRED 4-STAR GENERAL.

Now let's look at the happiness element.

This is much more subjective than the time element. But the sort of questions you need to be considering are:

- How often do I smile/feel appreciated/feel a warm-fuzzy glow at work?
- How often do I *want* to go the extra mile for
   a) my own pride?
   b) my colleagues?
   c) my customers?
   d) my boss?
- How often do I look forward to going to work in the morning?
- Are Monday mornings fun? Or Hell?
- Do I actually think 'Thank God it's Friday'?
- Would I recommend my place of work to my mates/children?
- Would I attend my boss's funeral to make sure the b*****r was dead or out of respect and affection?
- How proud am I of my uniform/liveried work wear/business card?
- How happy am I to answer that ever-present question in social situations, 'What do you do for a living?'

- How much of my holiday entitlement do I take?

- How much am I looking forward to retirement so that I don't have to see this place any more?

Next take the same sort of view of your life away from the workplace.

- How happy am I with my home?

- How much do I look forward to getting home at the end of the working day?

- What is it that I am looking forward to at the end of the day

  a) seeing my partner?

  b) seeing my mates?

  c) seeing my children?

  d) seeing my parents?

  e) seeing my dog/cat or other pet?

- How much are they looking forward to seeing me?

- Or is it *EastEnders* I am looking forward to seeing? Or the bottom of a glass?

- How full of enjoyment are my weekends (which may revolve around cleaning out the gutters if that floats your boat!)?

- Am I able to afford to take the kind of holiday I enjoy/drive the sort of car I'm not embarrassed to be seen in?

(You'll note that some of these questions relate to the outcomes of your work; they relate to your affluence or lack of it. This is not to suggest that money is the key to happiness, far from it, but if you hanker for more than your job/career provides you are likely to be unhappy.)

CASE STUDY

A young non-commissioned officer in the army had always hankered to buy a brand new Porsche on the day the new registration plate was issued. He and his wife had saved and dreamed and so, on the appointed day, he arrived at the barracks in a shiny new red 944.

In order to keep it pristine he put plastic bags over his army boots before he got in. He always parked it right outside his office window so he could keep an eye on it. After about three weeks he put it on the market; he was so stressed at the thought of his pride and joy, which represented such a large proportion of his worldly wealth, getting damaged that it was making him unhappy.

Once you have thought through and written down your answers to these questions, ask yourself an overriding question:

> *'Do these answers make me happy or am I significantly unhappy about the outcome?'*

If you are not satisfied with the time element, and the happiness element is not making you happy, then you really need to change something!

WORK/LIFE BALANCE ADJUSTMENT

"We can all be happy in a heartbeat if we make the decision to be so." INGRID COLLINS, CONSULTANT PSYCHOLOGIST, LONDON MEDICAL CENTRE.

A small amount of unhappiness is good; if humans had been happy eating raw meat off the bone and being cold then we would never have invented fire and would still be living in caves. Too much unhappiness is generally not good for us:

- it affects our physical health (we are worried sick or suffering from depression);
- it affects our relationships (other people avoid us because we just suck the joy out of their lives too);
- it affects our careers (we don't get promoted because we are seen as negative or miserable);
- it affects our families (we are the miserable negative parent/the ungrateful child).

And all of this affects the quality of our own life . . .

If you want to adjust your work/life balance you have two areas that you can change:

1 External areas: change your job, change your career, change your home environment.

2 Internal areas; change yourself, your attitudes, your outlook, your wants, your aspirations.

Making these changes can be started by going back to Chapter 3 and reassessing your answers there.

Read it and reap activities

Read the book *Soulwork, Finding the Work You Love, Loving the Work You Have*, by Deborah Bloch and Lee Richmond (1998), Palo Alto, CA: Davies-Black Publishing.

While you read the book, reflect on what you learn from it. When you have finished, take a short while to consider and write down the five main things that you have gained from the read. Which of these elements would you deem worthy of passing on to others? Write a brief 'review' of the book. If you want to, post this on a website such as **amazon.com** or a book club review site.

Read the book *Thank You*, by Liggy Webb (2011), Grosvenor House Publishing Limited.

While you read the book, reflect on what you learn from it. When you have finished, take a short while to consider and write down the five main things that you have gained from the read. Which of these elements would you deem worthy of passing on to others? Write a brief 'review' of the book. If you want to, post this on a website such as **amazon.com** or a book club review site.

CHAPTER 5

What's your brand?

WHY IT MATTERS

Unless your chosen career is 'hermit' you are going to rely on other people choosing you either as their supplier or their employee. Even lighthouse keepers have to get the job at the outset.

Your 'brand' is the image that other people have of you. You may have deliberately chosen the image you emit, or it may have evolved without conscious effort on your part. But, in the end, their perception is their reality . . . and it affects you.

"Your 'brand' is what people say about you when you're not in the room." JEFF BEZOS, FOUNDER OF AMAZON.

CASE STUDY (PART 1)

I was working with Chris, a middle manager, who was losing his job in a large government-owned scientific institution. He was monstrously well educated with two first-class degrees, a Masters and a PhD. And he had been successful in his civil service career, proving his technical ability in computer modelling of aerospace structures and propulsion systems. He had also been successful in developing novel computer simulation software to educate non-scientists in the development of rocket telemetry. He was, in short, a 'rocket scientist'!

At six foot three and eighteen stone he was a noticeable figure. He cut his own hair, bathed and shaved once a week, bit his nails down to the quick and generally wore a suit jacket, grubby tee shirt, crumpled chinos and sandals (he had in-growing toenails and found shoes uncomfortable), often with non-matching socks. He carried any papers he needed in a supermarket carrier bag and every pen in the universe in the breast pocket of his suit jacket.

He wanted to move into a role in educational software development and sales with a major computer consultancy in the UK or the USA. He was looking at a role with a base salary of c. £60k. He had already had several first interviews but no second interviews or job offers when I first met him.

He couldn't understand why, with his education and experience, he wasn't getting offers.

He needed to take a leaf out of Robert Burns' poetry:

O would some Power the gift to give us
To see ourselves as others see us! TO A LOUSE

He simply didn't look like a £60k consultant from a Big Five practice.

CASE STUDY (PART 2)

Chris and I had a session where we discussed personal branding and in particular the physical manifestation of appearance.

The next time I saw him he was clean-shaven, wearing a suit and polished shoes, a smart business shirt and tie and carrying a portfolio.

The very next interview he went to resulted in a second interview and then a presentation and then a job offer.

He had found a personal brand that aligned with his career goals.

Even those who ultimately make a point of bucking the brand issue have problems to overcome. There is a (possibly apocryphal) story of a young man walking up to the reception desk at County NatWest merchant bank and announcing that he had an appointment to see the head of Corporate Finance; the receptionist looked him up and down and said, 'Not dressed like that you haven't' . . . so the young, would-be entrepreneur walked away. His name . . . Richard Branson.

Personal branding isn't just about your dress and grooming. It encompasses every area where you leave a 'footprint'.

UNDERSTANDING YOUR CURRENT BRAND IMAGE

Consider where you create a footprint that a prospective employer or customer might see. Start closest to you and work away:

1 Your physical appearance:
   a) your grooming: head hair, facial hair, styling and condition;
   b) your skin: tattoos, piercings, fingernails, cleanliness;
   c) jewellery: rings, chains, watch, badges;
   d) clothes: style, colour, fit, cleanliness;
   e) shoes: style, condition, cleanliness;
   f) your teeth: shape, colour, gaps, cleanliness;
   g) your smell: scent/aftershave, tobacco/alcohol, body odour, work/hobby-related smell (dog/cat/exhaust/wood smoke/dry-cleaning fluid);

h) your gestures and physical mannerisms: fidgeting, eye contact, posture, stance, handshake.

2 Your voice and words:

a) your volume: does it create an image of confidence or shyness?

b) your tone: do you sound as if you are whining or angry or resigned or proud?

c) your 'quantity' of output: does this portray you as a motor mouth or the strong, silent type?

d) your accent: national or regional . . . it may be politically incorrect, but we are constantly bombarded by studies that show that people assume certain characteristics and personality traits from our accents. For example, research by Bath Spa University found that a Yorkshire accent was perceived as indicative of a higher level of intelligence than either received pronunciation or a Birmingham accent;

e) your grammar and pronunciation: what impression does yer talkin' voice give the pun'er, innit?

f) your language and choice of words: your opening gambit, 'Hae d'ye dooo?' or 'Wotcha, mate!'. Do you use the correct words or malapropisms? Do you pepper your speech with expletives? Is that appropriate for your situation?

g) your ability to articulate.

3 Specific 'documentation' you may have sent the person:

a) your business card/brochure: if you are representing an organisation then this speaks for you and the organisation (even if you ARE the entire organisation!);

b) your CV/résumé: is it traditional or modern, is there a photo on it, what is the colour and typeface?

c) your covering letter: what is your handwriting like and what image does this give, have you typed it, is the spelling and grammar correct?

4 Your virtual presence:

a) LinkedIn: are you? Is it up to date? What does it say about you?

b) Facebook: does this portray the image you want?

c) Friends Reunited: as above;

d) Twitter: do you tweet? If so what?

e) any other social networking sites;

f) your own website, 'vanity' or corporate;

g) your voicemail greeting on your work and private and mobile phones: your own voice? Short and sweet or rambling?

h) any special interest forum you may belong to;

i) your employer's website;

j) any press/media mentions of you.

Points a–g are predominantly self-developed, but also look out for comment from others that will come up if a search is done of your name.

Remember that if you have photos uploaded online, either on your own website or a social media network, they give an impression just as much as your actual appearance within eyeshot of a person. So try to look at these with an outsider's eye; what might they say about you? Not just your form of dress but also the overall scene; what is in the background, where was the picture taken, who else is in it? What impression could this give?

5 Also consider your forename or given name; what is the image that your forename may conjure up?

   a) are you Nicola, Nick, Nicky or Nicci? Do you write it with a ☺ over the i?

   b) are you a Mick, Micky, Mike, Mikey or Michael? Do you write it with a ☺ over the i?

   c) do you still use a childhood name into adulthood, such as Liggy Webb (Elizabeth), the author, or Bear Grylls (Edward), the survivalist?

6 And what about your surname or family name? We aren't looking at 'nominative determinism', whereby if your surname is Chua you should become a dentist or if your surname is Carr you should go into the automotive trade, but rather the issue of the ease with which potential employers may be able to pronounce your name. Joint research by the New York University's Stern School of Business and Melbourne University has found some interesting trends. People with more easily pronounceable names (regardless of the length of the name, the familiarity or the ethnic origin) get hired and promoted more quickly than people with names that managers and recruiters find to be tongue-twisters.

Now ask others to give you *their* impressions of your brand:

   a) someone who doesn't know you that well: ask this person to give opinions based on points 1–4 on the previous pages;

b) a personal friend: again ask them to give you opinion based on all the areas, but allow for the effect of their prior knowledge of you;

c) a work colleague or acquaintance.

These are quite big asks but they are worthwhile.

UNDERSTANDING THE BRAND IMAGE YOU NEED FOR THE CAREER YOU WANT

Having done some self-assessment of the reality of your current brand, you now need to look at your career objectives and assess what brand is appropriate for the type of career you want. Look at the categories in 1–4 above and ask yourself what brand will help you in this and what brand will hinder . . . or does it actually matter?

Look at people who are successful in the field you want to work in.

Look at the overall image of the companies/organisations that you would want to work for or with. Are they portraying themselves as economy, premium or luxury brands?

Look at the 'careers' page of their websites; what type of people do they say they are looking for?

Look at job advertisements and 'Person specifications'.

Build a composite list of the 'brand values' that are most likely to lead to success in your chosen field.

Rebranding yourself

Egalitarians will object to this activity: we should be judged for our ability and our skill rather than our appearance, and yes, they are right, we should. But very often we are not. We all have prejudices. Prejudices help us to make good decisions as well as bad ones. If a person claiming to be a motor mechanic comes to our door offering an 'at-home' auto tune-up but he has immaculately clean finger nails, a three-piece Armani suit and hand-made loafers we would be ill-advised to hand him our car keys. Similarly, if you wanted to (and could afford to) buy an Aston Martin and you went to their dealership and the sales receptionist looked as if she'd been dragged through a hedge, and swore like a character on *EastEnders,* you would probably give it a miss!

Our 'natural' prejudices have been harnessed wonderfully into the world of advertising. Go to YouTube – this is well worth one minute and thirty-nine seconds of your time . . . **http://www.youtube.com/watch?v=RS3iB47nQ6E**

I'm not suggesting you morph yourself into a different person, or put on a big act. Part of being successful is being authentic. But by being aware of this stuff you can work with it and use it to your advantage to accentuate the bits of your brand that fit with your desired career, or make an effort to change the elements of your current brand that might otherwise hold you back.

CASE STUDIES

Steve had been a welder on oil rigs for 13 years, his technical expertise was unsurpassed and his ability to teach, both welding and other subjects, was excellent. He wanted a change, a move to 'tie-wearing activities' in the company's training department. He recognised that his cultural habit of punctuating his effing speech with effing expletives all the effing time might make him effing acceptable on the rough, tough North Sea rigs, but it might be an effing hindrance in the London HQ. So he taught himself to jolly well stop swearing!

Benjamin Charles Elton is an educated man (grammar school in Godalming, Surrey, college in Stratford-upon-Avon) of impeccable middle-class background (son of a professor and a teacher, nephew of a noted and knighted historian). But it suited his 'alternative comedian' career choice to 'ave a bit more stree' cred, so 'e dropped 'is aitches an' dressed darn a bi' for his righ'-on, lef'-wing, Thatcher-bashing staaaand-up show. And he called himself 'Ben'.

Comedian Sandi Toksvig, on the other hand, is a Dane whose early education was in the United States, and when she first came to the UK she had not only a strong American accent, but also used American terminology. She taught herself to speak with received pronunciation in order to fit in at the public school she went to when her parents were posted to the UK.

WHAT'S IN A NAME?

Thespians and singers often select a name to suit their 'brand' – such as Madonna (who dropped the rest of her name: Madonna Louise Ciccone), or Seal (who also dropped the rest of his birth name Seal Henry Olusegun Olumide Adeola Samuel), or Joyce Penelope Wilhelmina Frankenberg who became actress Jane Seymour. We ordinary mortals don't have to go this far, but it is worth thinking about the real name you use:

- Do you drop a title? Viscount Stansgate became Anthony Wedgewood Benn.

- Do you adopt, or drop, a double-barrelled surname? Anthony Wedgewood Benn became Tony Benn.

- Do you make a name easier for 'indigenous people' to pronounce: Issur Danielovitch, or И´сер Даниело´вич, became Kirk Douglas when he joined the US Navy.

- Do you keep the correct ethnic pronunciation or spelling of your given name or make it easier for the local market? Like *Chris* Akabusi . . . no, he really is 'Kriss'.

- Do you deliberately make your surname name sound more 'exotic' by adopting a foreign pronunciation/spelling, e.g. Rogers to Rougier?

- Or do you anglicise it to make you fit in better? Saxe Coburg Gotha became Windsor.

- If you are born with a name that now has a connection to someone or something potentially embarrassing, do you change it? E.g. O'Rear becomes O'Riordon.

Like the chap in the earlier case study, you need to consider dressing and grooming for where you are going rather than where you are today.

If you feel that you need to make radical changes to your physical image, or you really are at a loss to know what to do to make the changes you think are necessary, then consider getting image makeover advice from a professional. There are a range of consultancies, just use an internet search engine to look for 'image consultants'; there is even a professional body to police the industry.

Read it and reap activity

Read *The Image of Success: Make a Great Impression and Land the Job You Want*, by Lizandra Vega, 2010, Amacom.

While you read the book, reflect on what you learn from it. When you have finished take a short while to consider and write down the five main things that you have gained from the read. Which of these elements would you deem worthy of passing on to others? Write a brief 'review' of the book. If you want to, post this on a website such as **amazon.com** or a book club review site.

MAINTAINING YOUR BRAND IMAGE

Keep your CV and online profiles current and updated as they are part of your constantly evolving brand image.

Also remember that the image you portray may need to change temporarily to reflect other elements of the situation.

CASE STUDY

A journalist told me yesterday how she had worked on a piece for BBC News to mark Armistice Day. She was to go and interview war veterans and record their stories about fallen comrades and then film the remembrance service at the Cenotaph. The veterans were wearing their carefully pressed uniforms and her piece was to convey the dignity and respect of the occasion. She had with her a university graduate who was doing some work experience. Work experience to get into TV is like gold dust and this was a great opportunity to be involved in a live project. The journalist turned up to interview the veterans only to be disappointed and shocked by how the graduate was dressed – short shorts with tights, a pair of boots and a scruffy top.

The graduate got it wrong and it cost her dearly. She was kept out of sight and not invited to be involved in interviewing the veterans. Not only that, but she deeply embarrassed the journalist. What are her chances for next time? Not great unless she thinks first about the situation she is entering and what the people she is meeting expect.

It's not all about image, but getting it right opens doors. Getting it wrong can have them slammed in your face.

From Lucinda Slater's blog
'Communicating your brilliance'.

You need to be aware that different people will see your image through their own perception filters, so you must try to put yourself in their shoes and see yourself through their eyes.

Most people have two slightly different personas: their work persona and their off-duty persona. I was once in a discussion with a group of managers whose employer was facing a takeover bid by a competitor. They described the CEO of the predatory company as 'Darth Vader', declaring him to be a heartless and arrogant man who cared nothing for the welfare of other people. They were able to quote numerous incidents of evidence that supported their opinion. I actually knew him socially as a quiet and devoted family man with a ready wit and a pleasant demeanour.

See Chapter 12, 'Getting the word out there', which looks at creating a PR campaign to ensure that the right people see your image.

CHAPTER 6

Family: fitting your lifestyle/career with theirs

TODAY AND TOMORROW

You may already have a family or you may be young (?), free and single. The likelihood is that, regardless of your gender, religion or age, at some stage you are going to have to take into account the needs of some element of 'family'.

This may simply be taking into account a partner or spouse (who may have their own career commitments), it may be considering their children and/or children you have together. It may move on to include your parent(s) and/or your spouse/partner's parent(s); and that may simply involve being in the same country as they are, so you can see them and they you, or it may include actually having some or all of them living in the same dwelling as you if you (or your partner) take on a caring role. Or you may decide to share a home for financial reasons, rather than a caring necessity.

When looking at the career element here it is vital to address several areas.

The career

a) Is the *career path* you wish to follow one that is likely to be 'supportive' of a happy family life? You need to look at this on a day-to-day basis:

1 are the *hours* you work going to create difficulties (40-hour week or a 90-hour week)?

2 is the time of day you are at work going to create difficulties (9 to 5, 7 to 7, alternative shifts and/or split shifts)?

3 is there an expectation that you will live on-site and therefore be available 24/7?

You need to look at this on a longer-term basis; is there a change of working pattern in the future, as I become more experienced/rise in the hierarchy, which might be beneficial or detrimental to my success/happiness as a family man or woman?

For example:

- A career in high-street banking will allow you to work in almost any town in the country, it allows you to work relatively regular hours and seldom requires 'antisocial hours'. It is reasonably safe (you are unlikely to be assaulted or killed at work) and uncontroversial (your family are unlikely to be publicly ashamed of your job.)

- A career in retail will allow you to work in almost any town, the hours are often shift work and there is a regular need to work Saturdays and Sundays. It isn't particularly dangerous or controversial either.

- A career in catering or hospitality often requires split shifts (e.g. cooking breakfast and dinner with the middle of the day and the late nights free) as well as weekend and bank holiday working.

- A career as a bailiff requires you to travel on a daily basis, it is a potentially dangerous role and is generally seen as quite controversial.

- A career in the armed forces is likely to require you to spend considerable stretches of time away from home, it will also require that your entire family relocate fairly regularly, it is potentially dangerous to life and limb and swings from respected to neglected depending on the political climate.

- A career as a professional sportsperson requires seven-day-a-week dedication and the possible need to relocate to the facilities or the club that are available. It will probably be a short-lived career once you reach a certain age, but the fame and glory are likely to be a source of pride to your family.

- A career in management consultancy for a big player in the market often provides an excellent salary and prospects, but this is sometimes tempered by having to live in hotels from Sunday night to Friday night for 50 weeks of the year. Even in five-star hotels this suits some people but not others!

b) Is your chosen career going to financially support a family?

- Is the *amount of money* you earn going to be enough to allow you to provide or contribute to the family finances?

- Is the *security* of the career adequate to 'bank on' in the future? In 2010 it was reported that raising a single child in the UK cost the parents between £117,700 and £220,800 from birth to the big 21st birthday; that is an average of over £5,500 per year, every year.

CASE STUDY

Jan reached the end of her university studies doing a BSc in Civil Engineering and started looking around for a first career opening. She discovered that, at the time, civil engineers were not that highly paid and that the industry was in the doldrums and lots of experienced civil engineers were being laid off. This got her thinking about consistency of need for employees. She concluded that there were only three areas of employment that were recession proof:

- audit accountancy/tax collecting . . . but she found these potentially boring;

- food production and retailing . . . but she found these uninspiring;

- cutting people's hair . . .

So she trained and then went to work as a hairdresser, and after seven years had a chain of salons and had earned her first million dollars!

c) Is the personality of your family members supportive of your hoped-for or current career?

For example:

- If your spouse/partner is emotionally (or physically) totally dependent on you then any career where you are away from home for any period of time is likely to put intolerable strain on the relationship.

- If your spouse/partner has a career that depends upon your active support then this can have a serious effect on your career (the spouses of army officers, vicars and MPs are often called on to perform supporting roles in an unpaid capacity.) And of course if your chosen career expects active support from your spouse/partner will they be prepared to give it?

- If your spouse/partner has a career/business interests that could embarrass you in your career there may be problems. E.g. you work for a government department and your spouse *works* as a political activist.

- If your spouse/partner has 'hobbies' that might cause embarrassment; these could be anything from environmental activism to amateur dramatics. A head teacher was embarrassed in the staff room when his wife appeared on stage in the town leisure centre (and the front page of the local paper) in her lingerie in an amateur production of *No Sex Please, We're British!*

- If your spouse/partner has a strongly held value or belief, such as 'don't put your daughter on the stage' or Rutherford's Law: 'there is no worthwhile human endeavour which benefits from the involvement of an accountant'.

Even before you have a specific career in mind it is worth giving consideration to these questions:

1 How long would you be prepared to work away from home, living in a budget hotel, in order to earn a good wage?

2 How would you react if your boss asked you to postpone your family holiday in order to carry out some important work for a client?

3 Would you prefer to

    a) turn down a promotion . . .

    b) or take the promotion and leave the family in your home country . . .

    c) or take the promotion and uproot the family and move half way around the world . . .

    for a three-year secondment?

4 In scenario c) above would it be different if

    a) you or your spouse were expecting a child

    or your offspring were

    b) toddlers,

    c) just pre-teens (10 to 12 years old),

    d) mid teens (14 to 17 years old)?

5 What would you do if it were a 10-month secondment?

6 What would you do if it were an emigration request to . . .

    a) a well developed and settled peaceful nation?

    b) a less developed, peaceful and stable but emerging nation?

7 How soluble would your concerns be in money (e.g. a tax-free salary double your present one)?

8 Would you be prepared to send your children to a boarding school if you were 'posted' to a country where they couldn't get a good education?

    What would you do if . . .

    a) they were reluctant?

    b) you wouldn't be able to see them during school holidays but they could stay with their grandparents?

9 Could/would you continue in your chosen career if your elderly parents needed you to provide them with some day-to-day help (not medical care but just shopping, driving them around etc.)

10 Who would *you* expect to put their career on hold if your child was seriously ill and needed constant parenting for several years, you or your partner? What is your partner's answer?

CHAPTER 7

Family *as* a career

Here is the controversial chapter; is being a parent actually a career? Is being a housewife/househusband or a mother or father actually a 'job'?

Evidence suggests that many people see this role as a non-job, of little relevance to the world of work.

CASE STUDY

I have recently started looking for a job after five years out of the workforce. Here are some of the responses I have been getting . . .

1 You haven't been working for five years

2 Your experience are (*sic*) not updated

3 Wow! Lucky you! Staying home!!

http://www.wifeadvice.com/2008/02/the-housewife-job-description/

Note that *even* the author of the comment refers to it as five years 'out of the workforce'. We almost all refer to a woman taking a 'career-break' to have children, so it is no wonder that there is a question mark over the matter.

Although biologically and historically women were the homemakers and men either couldn't or wouldn't, even this is taking a turn. In 1996, analysis by the UK Office of National Statistics found that 21,000 men categorised themselves as 'economically inactive and looking after the family or home'. By 2010 that figure had tripled to 62,000. This seems to have come about for several reasons:

- politically and socially it is more acceptable for men to be seen as househusbands;
- economically many more women now earn more than their male partners as equal rights legislation (and good sense) encourage more women into professional and managerial careers;
- more men want to take more of an interest in their children than perhaps was common in the past;
- traditionally male jobs have been perhaps harder hit by the economic changes in Britain away from heavy industry.

Interestingly, a recent survey for the insurance company Aviva suggests that over and above the 62,000 men who are actually 'economically inactive' there are a further 1.4 million men who are the main homemaker by dint of being self-employed and working from home.

Why might being a homemaker not 'count' as a job?

- You don't get paid for it.

- It isn't pensionable.

- There is no union protection.

- There is no 'professionalisation'; you can't get a BA or an MBA in Parenting Skills or Housewifery (you *can* get a qualification in 'Animal Husbandry' but the husbandry bit, thankfully, has a totally different meaning.)

- There are no employment rights.

- You don't get holidays.

- You don't get breaks.

- You are on 24-hour call out.

- There is no Working Time Directive.

- There are no incremental pay increases.

- There is no training available to help you do the job better. (Ok, there are actually dozens of organisations offering parenting classes, but for every person who recommends them someone else will say that they are rubbish!)

- Seldom do you get any recognition from your 'boss' (just once a year on Mothering Sunday or Father's Day).

So, from the point of view of common definition, being a homemaker or a parent doesn't count as a 'job' but is there anything more insulting than the question: 'Do you work, or are you just a housewife?'.

Being a homemaker, male or female, is a perfectly legitimate career choice, either temporarily (a short change of career from paid employment to parent in order to have and/or bring up children) or permanently. What could be more important to society than the development of the next generation?

As a homemaker you are responsible for many actions and outcomes:

- Hygiene in the home: this usually includes some of the inhabitants as well as the clothes they wear and the fabric of the dwelling.

- Nutrition: planning, sourcing, storing, preparing and presenting a varied and healthy diet for a range of ages, potentially from newborn to 100 years old.

- Sourcing all the content of the home: requiring consideration of the practical and utilitarian through to the aesthetic.

- Logistics: ensuring that there is adequate supply of all consumables but not an overstock problem that would either take up storage space or result in losses by wastage.

- Transportation: this usually requires considerable planning to ensure just-in-time delivery of different people to different places in a safe and secure manner while also ensuring economy in fuel terms and a degree of ecological consideration.

- Longer-term planning with regard to identification and securing of resources and facilities: this requires assessing schools' comparative suitability and understanding catchment area geography and policy.

- Health and safety: this ranges from the general safety around the house, access to dangerous objects and chemicals, to first aid and the issue of prescription and over-the-counter drugs. Also, providing the placebo and bedside manner most likely to achieve results.

- Diplomacy and peacekeeping: making peace between offspring or between offspring and other parent, and keeping that peace. Being seen to be fair and considerate at all times. Ambassadorial duties may be required relative to a partner's career and parents as well as to offsprings' friends and, in later times, lovers and partners.

- Therapy: you will doubtless have to act as a shoulder to cry on regarding your partner's career frustrations, and when your children begin to interact with others you will spend a fair amount of time listening to and advising them about relationships with their teachers, friends, enemies and secret passions.

- Teaching/learning support: life skills as well as homework/ coursework/assignments and projects.

- Fundraising: at some stage you are almost bound to be expected to raise funds for the pre-school, nursery, PTA, Cubs, Guides, Colts or similar.

- You may also find yourself at some point taking all these responsibilities for your parents, or your partner's parents.

- Budgetary management: ensuring that all stakeholders get fair treatment in the allocation of the household budget and that the budget is not exceeded.

- Scheduling: ensuring an even workflow of all of the above in spite of the unforeseen problems and tantrums that get thrown occasionally (or frequently).

As with all career choices there are downsides as well:

As a homemaker:

It can be hard to get out and make new friends. But most people in paid employment only make friends with work colleagues.

You can find that your topics of conversation become narrowed to children and home-related things. But most people in paid employment talk a lot of 'shop'.

You can find your profession-related skills get rusty. But most people in paid employment only update as regularly as their employer forces them to.

The most important person's opinion is your own; if you believe that investing part of your life in your family is worthwhile then it is.

The internet has made it much easier to continue in an earning capacity while staying at home and rearing children. Just run a web search on the word 'mousewife' or 'mousewives' and you'll find that scores of people who stay at home are earning money (in some cases they claim enormous sums) by writing or online auction trading. According to a 2009 survey for Kodak, in the UK nearly half of stay-at-home mothers used the internet to earn extra money; 1:20 of these report that they earn in excess of £200 per month. On top of this number many others use craft skills and sell solely via the internet. Many trained and qualified professionals are now able to work flexible hours from home in PAYE employment using email, VoIP, video conferencing and webinars.

Remember also that a homemaker's career develops as well. If you become a homemaker in order to have and raise a family your new career goes through evolving phases:

a) The initial phase is a new child: broken nights, permanent attachment to the baby, rapid and exciting development of the baby's personality and abilities.

b) Parenting a toddler: the 'terrible twos', when you become far more safety conscious and anxious and frustrated.

c) Pre-school and nursery era: now you get *some* 'me-time' during the day while your child is being eased into its first educational experience.

d) The primary school years: when you get a greater amount of, and more regular, time without the offspring, but you may be under pressure to take a very active role in parent/teacher association activities. ('After all you don't have anything else to do, do you? It's not as if you have a job!') You'll also be more involved in ferrying your child to their after-school activities and hosting their friends at your home.

e) The secondary school era: when you may have a bit more time to yourself while school is open but you may have a greater commitment in the evening with the homework/coursework supervision/assistance. School holidays make a difference to your daily and weekly routines as well as changing the routine of life for your child.

f) The further education or early career years for your child: when they may well be still living at home but you are less committed in terms of time.

g) They fly the nest and suddenly you may feel that it is all over.

Of course, you may have more than one child so this career development may have another layer superimposed. Or you or your partner may have children from another relationship, which can add yet another layer of development.

If you become a homemaker to look after elderly parents then there are similar evolutions:

a) You may begin with your elder charges in relatively good health, requiring company rather than care; you have quite a lot of me-time but are committed to being around.

b) As time passes you may become more of a carer in a domestic sense, you may also be the primary transport provider and trips to the doctor or hospital may increase in comparison to trips to the shops.

c) Later you may become more of a health carer, as well as covering the domestic arena.

d) Ultimately you may be needed 'on-site' 24 hours a day.

e) Finally you will be hit with the emotional wrench of the inevitable and at the same time you may find yourself with a lot more time on your hands.

So, if you are seriously considering taking a period of your career as a homemaker, ask yourself the following questions:

■ How will we ensure that the household income will be adequate to allow me to concentrate on being a homemaker?

■ How will I put money in my bank account/purse/wallet? (Many people find it psychologically very hard to have to actually ask their (earning) partner for money for house-keeping or little luxuries.)

■ How will I feel if I go for several days without face-to-face adult company?

- How much support will I get from my partner in my career in the same way that my partner will expect my support in theirs? Both practical support and emotional support.

- How resilient am I in the face of someone refusing to be reasonable (either your toddler or your parent/parent-in-law)?

- What will I do for intellectual stimulus as my homemaker responsibilities change?

- What kind of safety net is there in the event that I have to 'take a day off sick'?

- Am I able to take pride in a job 'well done, but unappreciated', such as cleaning out the loo?

- How can I ensure that I don't grow to resent my partner's apparent success in their career?

- What will I do in the event that the relationship with my partner goes sour (for money and for somewhere to live)?

- What is my exit strategy? This is a big one – if you become a full-time parent homemaker at 25 and your children leave home when they are 25 you will only be 50 years old when you 'retire' from that element of your role as homemaker; will you start another career at this stage or will you want to/be able to afford to retire to become a 'citizen of leisure'?

CHAPTER 8

The evolution of your career; can you future-proof it?

There are two distinct elements to future-proofing your career: internal aspects and external aspects.

- The internal aspects are self-driven: the way your career *wants* may change and develop and your *personal capacity* may change as you go through life.

- The external aspects are driven by others: the way a job, an organisation or an entire industry may change.

As you can imagine, you have a higher degree of personal control and influence over the internal aspects than the external, so we will look at these first.

INTERNAL ASPECTS – WANTS

It is fairly obvious that the things you want as an 18-year-old school leaver or a 21-year-old graduate may not be the same things that you want when you are 35 and settled with children.

- As a younger person you may crave excitement, physical challenge, constant variety and an enervating lack of security, whereas . . .

- Later in life you may crave intellectual challenge, a few more creature comforts and a higher degree of calm and security.

- At the age of 20 you may have no desire at all to teach others, whereas at 55 you may well get a huge amount of satisfaction from imparting your wisdom and helping others to learn and grow.

"Don't expect to choose the 'right' career straight away, and don't assume that changing it means that you're indecisive in your career choice or that you are a quitter." ROBERT WEEKS, OPERATIONS SUPPORT MANAGER, GRADWELL.

Look back at the list of likes and wants that you developed in the activities in Chapter 3. Some of the questions there were aimed specifically at looking at this aspect of future-proofing, where they asked you to consider some of the 'what ifs'. Now look at them again with an eye specifically to planning for the changes that might occur.

Again use the day-to-day and the outcome differentiators to consider how your likes might change/have changed as you mature and age. Consider the 'phases' of your life and the transitions from one to another:

- footloose and single;
- in a happy relationship;
- in an unhappy relationship;

- becoming a parent;

- getting older and less agile;

- getting bored/finding life too easy (this is called a 'velvet rut' and there is a whole section on this later in the chapter);

- planning for retirement.

Your list of life likes and wants can change very quickly based on real-life experience; you only have to look at the people who hanker after something for years, get it, find it just doesn't match up to their expectations and then their whole outlook changes. It can be a shock!

CASE STUDY

Harry Hill, television comedian, spent years training to be a doctor but didn't last long in the profession because, among other reasons, '. . . *seeing death happen was the worst thing, that will never leave me*'.

Sundaymercury.net, 28 February 2010.

Is your list of wants and likes still valid or have you moved on?

Getting the most from the present . . . for the future

The primary objective here is about seeing opportunities for the future from present activities. Let's take an example.

Present activity	Opportunity for the future
Tom is a 25-year-old with a zest for adventure who has saved up to take part in a round-the-world sailing challenge. He spends seven months aboard a clipper circumnavigating the globe. He is having a whale of a time and doesn't seem to be doing any more than having another gap year.	Tom is blogging daily about the experience and especially about what he learns about himself and others. Tom is carefully making a record of the contact details of all the people he meets, on his boat, on other boats and in each port they visit. Tom is keeping a pictorial record of all the activities aboard the ship, the places they go and the things he sees.

How is this helping?

a) The blog can be helpful in many ways; not only is it a way for family and friends to see what you are up to, but it is also potentially a money-spinner if posted somewhere where it can earn revenue via advertising. Not only would you be demonstrating your writing ability, but also learning about and demonstrating your transferable skills in blog marketing and online advertising. While not quite a travel blog, the young Brooke Magnanti made a great financial success of her extracurricular blog; to the point of it becoming a money-spinning best seller alongside her medical career. See **http://en.wikipedia.org/wiki/ Belle_de_Jour_(writer)**

Having the discipline to keep the blog updated will also teach Tom the benefits of time management and show him that when you keep a record of what you are doing it is easier to reflect on and consider what it is that you have learned. This in turn will reinforce the learning (making it learning by intention rather than learning solely by intuition) and tends to remind you just how much you are learning as well. This can be important to your self-esteem, as extracting the learning from any situation gives value even to the most spectacular failure; if you aren't earning at least learn.

b) By collecting the contact details of the people he meets, Tom is building his first network. He has discovered that the world is full of interesting and potentially useful people and the more people you meet and keep in some sort of contact with, the better. If you are ever in a similar situation it is always worth having some 'calling cards' ready to hand out. These are like a business card, *without* organisational name and/or title but with your *personal* contact details:

Jean Doe

jdoe@yahoo.dot   07777 1234456

Not only does this give you something tangible to pass on to anyone but the act of giving it, in most cultures, suggests a need for reciprocity; you don't have to ask for someone's contact information, they will tend to feel that they want to give it.

c) The pictorial record may be valuable in several ways:

- It is a great memory jogger for the networking element; it puts a name to a face and a face in a place (in geography and time).

- Pictures are also marketable; it can help your blog by adding a visual dimension.

- When you are old and grey it will liven up your life story for your grandchildren!

- If you are a good photographer and are lucky/skilled enough to get some great shots, they may form the basis of a coffee table book!

What Tom is doing is twofold. He is actively using his 'spare' time productively and he is developing an appreciation of his 'transferable skills'. Tom is doing this while he is engaged in a 'jolly', but it can be done while you are doing your day job, doing an extracurricular job, pursuing a hobby or interest. Transferable skills mean that you can take learning from your part-time job as a waiter to the Customer Service department of BT, or from your job as the Marketing Manager for Lloyds TSB to running a bookshop in darkest Totnes.

Beware the 'velvet rut'

You have probably heard the term 'stuck in a rut' . . . it relates to that situation where you may want to change something but the wheels of your life are 'stuck in a rut' – you just can't seem to change course. This is most often used to describe a situation relating to a bad habit, such as smoking or drinking too much, or having to face the consequences of former actions, such as having built up large debts.

The term 'the velvet rut' was coined by Harold Ross, the founder of *The New Yorker* magazine, who is reported to have said of his publication at one stage, 'We're in a velvet rut – by which I mean the stuff is pretty average, but we're making money out of it.' Many people's careers get in the same situation: they are dull and lifeless but changing is difficult, and the reason it is difficult is because they are very comfortable.

CASE STUDY

For 22 years I worked at a consulting engineering company, for the same boss in pretty much the same role. Nothing much changed in all that time, except that my comfort zone became even more comfortable. Then my husband got a two-year assignment to China and I went with him. As I did not have a work permit I suddenly found myself at a total loose end, which I found incredibly frustrating.

So I decided to take a life coaching course. I loved it. Now all I needed was to put the tools I had learnt into practice. But where was I going to find clients? Then a brainwave struck and I started a Support and Friendship Club for Expat Women in Shanghai. I advertised on the Expat website, and put out the word. Pretty soon I was in contact with a number of interested women, and we had our first meeting. It didn't take long for the word to spread and within a short space of time we had 100+ members and I found myself coaching women from all over the world – Russia, Australia, New Zealand, Malaysia and Japan, to name but a few.

The human resources department at my husband's company were aware of my adventures and so when we returned home they quizzed me about what I intended doing with my future. As a result of this I negotiated a job offer as an International Assignments Advisor, which provided me with untold opportunities to use my life coaching skills.

After two years in the role a new opportunity arose, one that made me realise what really makes my heart beat faster – I became an Employment Assistance Programme Champion, a role that I find so fulfilling. I have also registered my own training and development business and spend some time mentoring younger people.

Work is now my hobby and every day is challenging and different. I do not think I could be more fulfilled career-wise if I tried. But this life I have created started thanks to fate more than anything else. I can't imagine how dreary my life would be if I was still in that original job.

Now when I am talking to people my first piece of advice is: don't limit yourself. There's a world of opportunity out there for you to explore, and ensure that you reach your full potential. After all – eagles must leave the nest in order to spread their wings . . . I did, and life is pure joy.

Carrol Roberts-Harrison,
EAP Specialist at Hatch, South Africa

Many people in public sector jobs or jobs with big, well-established businesses are stuck in a rut. They are no longer happy with either the day-to-day work they do, or the environment they work in. They are bored to death, unchallenged and learning nothing, but at the same time they are well paid, well benefitted and unlikely to have problems with their performance due to their familiarity with both the job and the internal politics of the organisation.

You may be stuck in a velvet rut if you are unfulfilled but feel that you cannot change course for some reasons. These reasons may range from:

- hanging on for the pension;
- having now branded yourself so strongly in your current successful persona that you feel you couldn't reinvent yourself;
- being so completely settled into certain working time patterns/locations that changing to different patterns would be too uncomfortable (think MPs, academics, shift workers, Expats);
- having had consistent incremental pay rises you now couldn't afford to start again in a new career;
- the fringe benefits are such that no other role would match them (on-site gym, subsidised medical care and so on);
- your family have a dependence upon the benefits of your career and the upheaval would be too great if you made a change at this stage. This could be anything from your spouse on your medical cover to your children in boarding school on a fee support-programme.

Future-proofing if you are in (or are likely to get into) a velvet rut

First let's be clear, a velvet rut isn't necessarily a bad place to be. Many of the people who devote a huge amount of time to charity, social and environmental activism and help and support to others are able to do so solely because they are in a velvet rut. It is a form of the noblesse oblige that used to motivate many upper-class and upper-middle-class Victorians to such great philanthropy.

If, however, you are concerned at being trapped in a velvet rut there are some actions that you can take to avoid being made unhappy by it:

1 Do something about your job itself.

Think laterally about the parameters of the actual job you do – what responsibilities could you propose adding to give the job some challenge. These could include:

- setting more demanding goals within the current job description;
- dedicating energy to the development of the people below or around you (this could involve your subordinates, customers, suppliers or peers);
- publicising the profession, organisation or discipline, for example school/university careers liaison, or being a 'brand ambassador'.

2 Do something about your happiness level out-of-hours.

Think laterally about your values (see Chapter 2) – what activities could you engage in, *alongside your current role*, that would bring some challenge and happiness back into your life? These can be purely hobby related or can relate to some form of societal or professional benefit.

- Can you take a more active role in any trade or professional association (as a regional officer, a speaker or a membership recruiter)?

- Is there a local community organisation that would give you some stimulus and challenge (as an organiser, fundraiser, mentor or even labourer)?

- Is there a social or spiritual organisation that holds meaning for you (as an activist, member or chapter leader)?

- Is there a hobby or interest that you would like to pursue?

3 Do something about your level of knowledge and/or skill. This could relate either to your current career, a possible future career or just 'for the hell of it'.

- Could you enrol in a course or qualification that would qualify you to widen your career options in your current role? An MBA, an HGV licence, a professional qualification?

- Could you learn a new career-related skill that might open other doors for you, such as creative writing if you are currently an HR manager or interior design or web design if you are currently a shop assistant?

- Could you enrol in learning something that just interests you but which you have no intention of turning into an earning option? Such as pottery, or stained glass making, a foreign language or a game such as bridge or chess?

(While number 3 may not seem to be future-proofing your career as such, it is in a roundabout way; it increases your longevity in the current earning position by reducing the likelihood of throwing it over out of sheer boredom!)

4 Quit and find a new challenge!

Beware the 'affluence trap'

Another 'problem' area, with similarities to the velvet rut, is the affluence trap. The affluence trap is defined as the situation where a successful person, couple or family has all the material trappings of wealth and success, but the use of the term 'affluence' may be misleading. They are now committed to large regular payments (mortgage, HP, rental) and are therefore trapped in their unfulfilling job(s) as it is the source of their capacity.

Of course it is easy to say that people in this situation should or could simply divest themselves of the material trappings but:

- in recent years many people have been in the situation of negative equity with their mortgage;

- if you sell your expensive house and move to a cheaper one you undoubtedly have to relocate as well; this impacts on children's schooling (state or private), spouse's career and other family relationships;

- selling a house and moving to another costs a lot of money (2010 UK average was reported to be in the region of £11,000);

- HP on a car comes with a virtual guarantee of a negative equity situation for some years;

- most goods bought with credit cards are almost immediately worth less than the debt still owed on them.

Often we allow our social pride to prevent us from 'downsizing'; remember the foreman in the film *The Full Monty*? He couldn't bring himself to tell his wife that they could no longer afford to continue their lifestyle when he lost his job. Luckily(?) for him he didn't have to make a choice about breaking out of the affluence trap . . . he was forced to.

Future-proofing if you are in (or are likely to get into) the affluence trap

If you are in, or in danger of finding yourself in, the affluence trap then you are well advised to start discussing it with your spouse or partner sooner rather than later.

Read it and reap activity

Visit **http://www.greenuniversity.net/Green_ Economics/jobtrap.htm** and read the article and the response letters. The article is aimed at getting out of the affluence trap for the specific motivation of being environmentally responsible, but a very large percentage of the content is just as relevant to people who just want to live for themselves rather than their bank manager.

Reflect on what you have learned there that you may be able to put in place for yourself and your family.

INTERNAL ASPECTS – CAPACITY

CASE STUDY

Twenty-five years ago I was a member of a sport diving club. The club was run by a fire-fighter and a paramedic and those two employments were quite heavily represented among the membership. Last month I ran into one of the ambulance crew members. She still drives an ambulance but she is worried now that the economic situation means that she won't be able to retire at 60 with a full pension . . . she is finding it tough carrying stretchers up and down stairs at the age of 50 . . . the thought of doing so at 67 doesn't bear thinking about.

The reality of life is that we will probably be working well into our 60s (if not our 70s or even 80s if the economy keeps its current trends with regard to pensions and elder care). This being the case, we need to plan so that we will be doing less physical labour, less travelling around and taking on less stressful daily workloads.

There are several approaches we can adopt to help future-proof our life:

1 Choose a career where there is a clear career path that will allow you to *happily* move away from the more physically demanding side of the role. (The important word here is 'happily'; if you became a rigger because you love working at heights, then you may find that sitting in an

office planning rigging shifts bores you to death. Don't just look for management progression or income progression, look also at the happiness progression.)

2 Choose a career that will allow you to move out when you get to the point where you no longer have the capacity for the physical demands of the job. ('Out' could be to retire having made enough money – the goal of those professional footballers mentioned in Chapter 3. Or 'out' could mean to a related role, so the ambulance driver in the case study above could move into a teaching/training role for an ambulance service for instance.)

3 Choose a career where the physical element of the job is less important in the first place. (Remember that 'physical' may not solely be about your strength, speed or stamina, such as a sports person, fire-fighter or bricklayer, but it can also be about eyesight for an HGV driver, adaptability to different time zones for an international courier or flight attendant and psychological resilience for a prison warder or a customer complaint handler.)

4 Choose a 'career' that is, in itself, a stepping-stone to another opportunity more suited to you in later life.

EXTERNAL ASPECTS

Gone are the days of people completing an entire career in one organisation; even police and soldiers seldom see out a full 22 years and then *retire completely*.

Indeed, there are many arguments against the concept of single-employer careers:

- many recruiters, both agents and employers, start to question an individual who has remained with the same company for 20 years;

- remaining with one employer tends to reduce an individual's circle of acquaintances and co-workers;

- this is then particularly dangerous when two co-workers marry and their offspring end up joining the firm; a severe round of redundancy can then cost two or three generations their livelihood in one fell swoop;

- many 'company men' (and women) become terminal bores due to their limited topics of conversation;

- total reliance on one employer can be terminally dangerous; for instance, when Robert Maxwell's business went 'belly up', many long-term employees lost not only their jobs but also their pension funds.

Nowadays it is far more likely that you will have several separate part-careers, and this can be in three fundamental ways:

1 Several careers in *sequence,* which are linked and related.

For instance, you may start out as a retail assistant working in a high-street store and move up into a management position. From here you may move sideways into a merchandising role in a regional centre of the original employer. Then you may move to a more strategic merchandising and buying role for another retailer in their corporate head office. Then you may be headhunted to a retail consultancy.

2 Several careers in sequence that are not clearly linked or closely related.

For instance, you may begin with a short stint in a 'young person's' job in the armed forces. On completion of your contract commitment you may resettle into a sales position in financial services. When that has run its course you may move to a recruitment and selection consultancy and when the recruitment business is in the doldrums you may re-invent yourself as a trainer. Based on the experience you have gained you may then start writing books.

3 Several careers in parallel as a 'portfolio'.

After an initial few years in a corporate job you may set up a small internet-based trading business, which you run from home. At the same time you begin to develop an interest in property and buy a couple of buy-to-let flats in the local university town. As the property goes well you expand that portfolio up to five flats while still holding down a corporate job and getting a subcontractor to handle the bulk of the online trading business. You get made redundant from the corporate role but are quite quickly snapped up by another employer, a role you elect to take on a part-time basis so you can continue your property business.

Enforced redundancy is now the norm for pretty much everyone at some stage of their working life; there just isn't such a thing as a safe or secure job any more. Even in a career that society 'cannot do without', such as teaching or nursing, employers are finding ways to offshore the work or simply change the mechanics from employed to out-sourced or subcontracted.

The important element to remember is that in corporate employment you have virtually no personal control and precious little influence over the future of your employment. Consequently, if you want to ensure that you continue to eat and prosper you need to take control of that which you can control, rather than simply trusting to luck and having faith in somebody else, such as your boss or the human resources department. To put it in the terminology of a T-shirt or poster:

> *Do you want to make it happen?*
> *Watch it happen?*
> *Or ask,*
> *'What happened?'*

Many people who just got on with the job they were paid for found the sudden receipt of a P45 a very shocking and painful moment. And it was seldom short-lived pain; several months of unemployment is hard to handle, especially when you have a spouse and children and half the staff of your bank to support. Even with a good payoff it can be psychologically hard to take.

Many people do later report that getting made redundant was the 'best thing that ever happened to them' (oh, their spouse must be sooooo pleased! What about the wedding or the birth of their children?), but they usually then add the words, 'eventually' or 'after a couple of years' or 'looking back on it'.

"Never let your ego get so close to your position that when your position goes, your ego goes with it." COLIN POWELL, US STATESMAN AND RETIRED 4-STAR GENERAL.

This is an easy trap to fall into – here's how to avoid it:

- If you think of yourself as (and therefore introduce yourself as) a *bank manager*, and the bank makes you redundant . . . then you are nothing.

  Whereas . . .

- If you think of yourself as a *highly skilled person* who is *currently* a bank manager, then if the bank takes your job away, you are still a highly skilled person.

Future-proofing your career against a corporate redundancy

Please note that these are not policies to *prevent* you being made redundant, pretty much nothing (legal and moral) will achieve that; these are policies to *help you survive* in the event of being made redundant.

- Keep your résumé or CV up-to-date all the time.

- Keep some 'calling cards' to hand (as mentioned earlier in this chapter).

- Think of your CV in terms of the skills you use and the knowledge you possess; these things are transferable, whereas a job title may not be.

- Make sure that you keep your contact book personal, not 'company property'. This isn't suggesting that you steal; just that you make sure that, if you were locked out of your

PC and escorted from your desk tomorrow, you would be able to get in touch with suppliers, customers and industry contacts to let them know you are moving and available.

- Build some profile: get yourself on to social networking sites such as LinkedIn, MySpace, Facebook and so on (pick the ones that suit the relevant type of career).

- Keep these profiles in line with the image you should have and update them regularly. Lynda Gratton, Professor of Management Practice at London Business School, advises that though it is critical to use social networking sites to help future-proof a career, you have to be sensible – there is no point in having 1,000 'friends' on Facebook but no one to really talk to about your work. You need a potent balance of people to really support you in your career, and not all of them will be found on Facebook and LinkedIn.

- Do whatever you can to develop a reputation within the industry, trade, profession or locality that is appropriate . . . this is a great way to . . .

- . . . network with the type of people who may either want to offer you a job or a project should you become suddenly 'available'.

- *Always* scan the recruitment pages of the relevant press and websites; this keeps you up-to-date with who is active (agencies and recruiters), what types of job are on the up and what the salaries and benefits are like.

- If you get calls from head-hunters while you are working (or direct approaches from suppliers or customers) at least go along and talk to them; it isn't disloyal, it is sensible!

Read it and reap activity

Read The Shift by Lynda Gratton, 2011, Collins.

While you read the book, reflect on what you learn from it. When you have finished, take a short while to consider and write down the five main things that you have gained from the read. Which of these elements would you deem worthy of passing on to others? Write a brief 'review' of the book. If you want to, post this on a website such as **amazon.com** or a book club review site.

It is also relevant to bear in mind that 'outrageous fortune' can also make it impossible for you to continue in a particular job as a result of injury or illness. Anything from a major accident and resultant disability through to a serious illness can render a past career choice less viable. While we don't want to sink into a sea of depression considering the what-ifs of your becoming severely disabled or seriously ill, go online and search out the name Jean-Dominique Bauby and read a bit about what he achieved. Look up Simon Weston as well, another character whose strength in adversity is an inspiration.

"Work on doing what you want to do now, *because you may never get the opportunity again."* ANDREW JACOBS, LEARNING AND DEVELOPMENT MANAGER.

WHEN LIFE GIVES YOU LEMONS . . .

Sadly, life isn't fair; otherwise we'd all look like George Clooney or Audrey Hepburn, or we would all have been born into the Rockefeller or Gates family. So you might be perfect for that job and still not get it. Or you may have a great job and lose it, through no fault of your own. When life gives you lemons, you may be very tempted to:

- complain to everyone who will listen that life is unfair;
- argue the toss;
- attempt to reason with the agency, the recruiter, your employer or your boss;
- appeal to other people for sympathy or support;
- picket;
- blog about the iniquity of it all;
- even take legal action to get a job or keep your job . . .

In 99 per cent of cases this is a complete waste of time. Things change and change has implications that often are not fair; you can either spend time and energy fighting the inevitable or you can invest that time and that energy into looking for a new opportunity.

Read it and reap activity

Read the book, *Who Moved My Cheese?*, by Spencer Johnson, 1999, Vermilion.

This is a book that many people love and a few people really hate . . . but it will take about 45 minutes to read so it is worth the gamble.

CHAPTER 9

Soar with the egos

WHAT DO WE MEAN BY 'EGO'?

According to the lyrics of Flanders and Swann's old number 'Sounding Brass',

Society frowns upon blowing one's own trumpet.

But the sad reality is that no else is going to blow it for you. We can probably all think of at least one person about whom we think 'How on earth did they get that job?'. The simple answer is that it is not always the 'best 'person who gets the job, just the person who is best at getting hired.

The word ego is usually used in a slightly pejorative sense, but it is not a dirty word. Some people have a bit 'too much' of an ego, but the reality of life is that without one you simply will not succeed in whatever it is that you want to do or achieve.

The technical definition goes like this:

> *Your ego is your sense of self relative to others.*

We all have a level of self-interest that falls somewhere on the scale below:

Id				Ego				Superego
−4	−3	−2	−1	0	1	2	3	4
Total apathy to my own self-interest				A balance between 'me' and others				Total apathy to anyone else's interests

An extreme example of the −4 level might be committing suicide in the belief that I'm the most useless person on the planet.

At −3 it is possible that I may give up on myself, drop out of society and live by begging in shop doorways, because I am not worthy to receive more than the charity of others.

At −2 I may just accept any dead-end job but, being so convinced that I'm the worst person they could have given it to, I fail.

At −1 I may accept a dead-end job because I believe that this is 'the best I deserve'.

At 0 I may be going and getting the type of job I want and deserve.

At 1 I may believe I can be, or do, better (according to my own definition of 'better') and I strive to achieve this by dint of hard work and application.

At 2 I may be happy to work within a team for success and to take credit where it is due to me for that success.

At 3 I may be being prepared to take credit for other people's work in order to reap benefit to myself.

At 4 I may be being prepared to lie, cheat and stab other people in the back in order to achieve what I want.

'EGO' IS NOT A DIRTY WORD!

A sense of ego is a very healthy thing to have.

- It keeps you (and the human race) alive on a very basic level. Without any ego, you have no desire to live (and therefore no desire to continue the species).

- With an ego you endeavour to develop yourself as a person, while remaining considerate to those around you. You have, therefore, the capacity to be a contributing member of society.

- If you have 'too much' ego, i.e. superego, then you may be immensely successful on a financial/status/power basis but you may well be seen by others as a sociopath, someone who feels no empathy at all for anything beyond yourself.

Your ego state is directly linked to your self-esteem and this is not a fixed thing, it can change in response to your environment:

1 If you are constantly told that you are a worthless, then your self-esteem will probably be low and you will lose self-belief, leading you to either *continue* to fail (probably because you don't try as hard as you could, because, after all, there is no point, is there?) or you will *cease* to fail because you simply cease to try, again there is just no point, is there?

2 If you are constantly told that you *can* succeed *if* you try, that you just need to believe in yourself and put in the effort and the thought, then you will try and you may well succeed. And if you don't succeed you will probably try again, a little differently, until you do succeed.

3 If you are constantly told that you are wonderful and that everything you touch will turn to gold regardless of the effort and thought you put in, then you will start to believe it and your self-esteem will become so high that you will genuinely think that you deserve instant success without any effort or consideration. This means that you may well try anything, regardless of good sense or advice.

This is related to the 'self-fulfilling prophecy', and forms the basis of many of the policies used (or abused, depending on your opinions) in education in the developed world.

> *"Whether you think you can or think you can't – you are right."* HENRY FORD, FOUNDER OF THE FORD MOTOR COMPANY

WHERE WE GET OUR LEVEL OF SELF-ESTEEM

For many people, their self-esteem has taken a serious battering even before they get to leave school; their parents and their teachers may have damaged their self-esteem in one of two ways:

Too much 'love'	Too much 'criticism'
The parents do everything for their offspring, showering their child with every material reward they can (or even can't) afford. They protect their beloved from any form of failure, for instance by doing their homework for them, or giving them a sick note on sports day The parents or the school go out of their way to make excuses for 'poor' academic performance, even to the extent of having the child assessed for mild learning difficulties	The parents never appreciate anything that the child does, or at best constantly point out how things are easier than in their day They give no praise when the child does something right but only ever seem to notice when a detention slip comes home or something gets broken A sibling is always held up as the paragon of virtue and this child is always made to feel like an embarrassment Teachers only ever seem to criticise the child's work, 'nit-picking' over every small error without recognising the good work as well

Too much 'love'	Too much 'criticism'
The teachers allow them as many rewrites as they need to get their schoolwork done, there is no meaningful sanction for failing to do homework or coursework and 'deadlines' are almost infinitely flexible. Lavish praise is given for any act, regardless of how meaningless it is	Teachers denigrate the child as stupid or useless or 'not as good as your elder brother/sister' They perhaps refer to the entire class as being no-hopers, the 'worst I've ever taught'. Even worse, the teachers fall into the 'people like you/from this area have no hope at all because the economy is in the doldrums and the best you can hope for is the dole . . .'

Possible outcomes of too much 'love'

If parents do everything for their child, they create a cocoon of 'learned dependence' where the child develops no capacity to do anything for itself; this can range from a teenager's inability to tidy its own room, to the inability to cook themselves a decent meal, through to an inability to manage their own money, through to an inability to relate to strangers because of a combination of the constant protective chant of 'stranger danger' and the parental preference to have their child at home on the computer rather than out in the fresh air . . . where there are dangers!

What does this matter? It matters in one of two ways:

a) When the child/adult is first exposed to the independence of the 'real world' they fail and suffer severe damage to their self-esteem, which puts them at a sudden id level on the ego scale.

b) Or when the child/adult is first exposed to the real world and fails . . . they react with their learned superego – that the fault must be someone else's and not in any way theirs. Consequently, they start to 'take it out' on society, their neighbours, friends, co-workers.

Possible outcomes of too much 'criticism'

It is almost a simple cycle.

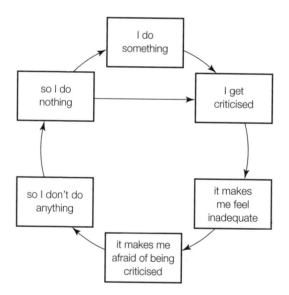

Of course, it isn't only in the early years that other people's attitudes affect our self-esteem; hen-pecked husbands, downtrodden wives, new recruits, are all examples of adults who are on the receiving end of feedback and comment from others that changes their level of self-esteem.

Senior managers, entertainment divas and long serving political leaders are also examples of people who get so much adulation and fawning that they begin to believe in their own invincibility.

WHAT'S GOING ON IN YOUR LIFE?

Take some time to consider the following question and the corresponding comments:

What does the 'little voice' inside your head generally sound like?

a) Is it telling you that you are probably wrong/going to fail/ without any hope?

b) Is it pointing out to you that life isn't fair and that everyone else is either out to get you or doesn't care about you?

c) Is it a voice that helps you to weigh up the pros and cons of your options?

Comment: Analysing what that 'little voice' says is an important part of understanding your own level of self-esteem. If your little voice tells you that you are powerless and deserve no better (a or b) then you are likely to go on through life being downtrodden and doing the bidding of others. If the little voice is asking you all the questions that help you to take rational decisions about your options (c), you are likely to find that you are able to act to build a happier life for yourself.

Are you doomed to *eternal* failure or do things *usually* go right for you?

Take some time to consider the following questions and the corresponding comments:

When you try something and it doesn't work out, what are you *more likely* to think?

a) Here we go again, same as always; nothing *ever* goes right for me!

b) Oops! That didn't work. I wonder what I could do to make it work.

Comment: We tend to categorise our failures and difficulties, successes and achievements as either *permanent* (a) or *temporary* (b). This often links to the criticism cycle on page 127; we have reached the point where we either believe that we will *always* fail or we believe that we can succeed, but perhaps not every time. If we believe we will always fail then we stop trying; when we stop trying we become failures.

Interestingly, this is not a holistic thing for most people; they may have found some aspect of their lives that they believe they can succeed at, hence they try and they succeed. In other areas of their life they believe that they cannot succeed; in these areas they either don't try, or they make a half-hearted effort but since, deep down, they believe that they are doomed to permanent failure, they fail.

> *'Sfortuna al gioco, fortuna in amore.'*
> As they say in Italian, or in English
> *'Unlucky at cards, lucky in love.'*

You only have to look at the celebrities who can act or sing but cannot keep sober/off drugs or in a stable relationship to see this in action.

Are you the architect of your own demise or just unlucky?

Take some time to consider the following question and the corresponding comments:

When you are dealing with a problem in your life, what are you *more likely* to think?

a) It isn't my fault, the timing/market/support/weather (anything other than you) was wrong.

b) Oh hell, if only *I* hadn't . . .

Comment: We tend to ascribe our successes and failures to factors that are either *internal* (b) or *external* (a). This is often referred to as our 'locus of control'. If you take an *internal* locus of control over your *failures/pains/problems*, you can end up damaging your self-esteem further. For instance, 'If only I hadn't chosen to go to work at 10 o'clock that drunk driver wouldn't have been there and I wouldn't have ended up in hospital. It's all my fault.'

You may have noticed that both the questions above asked what your most *likely* reaction was. For many people, they have a default setting in the way they see things:

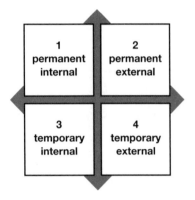

Having a default setting is potentially limiting since:

- if you always ascribe failure to your own actions then it tends to result in inaction;

- if you always ascribe failure to others you never improve your chances of turning the failure around;

- if you always ascribe your success to your own ability you come to believe in your own perfection;

- if you always ascribe your success to others you become dependent on others, or to chance.

And

- if you always ascribe your failure as permanent you will never succeed;

- if you always ascribe your failure as temporary you may keep failing when success is actually not possible;

- if you always ascribe your success as permanent you are likely to be in for a big shock one day!

- if you always ascribe your success as temporary you are unlikely to recognise that it was down to something that you may be able to replicate!

Take time to consider the occasions in the past when you have succeeded or failed; ask yourself whether you ascribed it at the time as permanent or temporary, to internal or external factors.

> Do you have a default setting, and if so what is it?

> Is any default setting common for all areas of your life or just some?

> Reassess some of those past successes and failures. Do you now see them in a different light?

> What effect might this have on your future efforts and activities?

(RE)ASSESSING AND (RE)BUILDING YOUR SENSE OF WORTH

If you have achieved things in your life then stand tall and be proud of them, don't hide your light under a bushel, remind yourself of them on a regular basis – it does wonders for your self-esteem.

If you have pictorial evidence as well, display it – let others see that you are an achiever.

- If you have a degree then put the post nominal letters BA or BSc on your business card, signature block of your emails, the top of your CV, your front door. If it's an Honours Degree then put (Hons) on there as well. If you have a photo of you in your mortar board being given your degree by the Chancellor, display it.

- If you are entitled to use the title 'Dr', then do so; you earned it.

- If you have been awarded a medal, then frame the citation and put it on your wall.

- If you have ever appeared in the press, keep a cutting, framed and visible.

- If you ran a marathon and have a picture of you crossing the finish line, frame it and display it.

- If you got a commendation at work, frame it and put it up (at home if you don't want it in the office).

- Be proud of what you have achieved, and what has been recognised by others.

Make a list of *all* your achievements, starting at primary school and working up to the present day. Don't be shy about it – no one else is going to see that you won the 'Mrs Joyful Prize for Raffia Work' at the age of three, or passed your Cycling Proficiency at the age of nine – but they are achievements that you have attained and they add to your stock in your own mind.

Don't confuse 'achievements' with 'qualifications':

CASE STUDY

Richard was being made redundant from a supervisory job in a heavy manufacturing industry and dearly wanted to work in the new industrial heritage centre that was opening in the town. His problem: he had never studied tourist management or curatorship, which were what was advertised as the must-have qualifications.

The fact that during Richard's working life he had been the archivist for the single largest collection of historic hand tools in Europe, had advised historical institutes on material conservation and had presented on two educational television documentaries completely slipped his mind!

Note: Many people are proud of what they are – their race, their nationality, their regional identity, their 'gang', their gender, their sexual identity or their class. While it is also perfectly acceptable to be proud of what you are, remember this comment from Sir Michael Caine, the cockney-born actor, who came from very humble beginnings to be an international star, millionaire and national treasure:

> 'When somebody says to me, "I'm proud of being a cockney", I say, "What else are you proud of?' What do you do?"'

His point, of course, is that what you *are* is little more than an accident of birth; what you *do* is what both defines you and makes people either respect you or ignore you or loathe you.

Caine has made over 100 films and is one of only two actors nominated for an Academy Award in every decade from the 1960s to 2000s (the other being Jack Nicholson). We know what he *does*, cockney or not!

It is hard to have a degree of ego or self-esteem if you don't feel that you have achieved very much. This can be a particular problem if you are only just out of college or school, if you are a late-developer, or someone who has been tied up in one all-encompassing job for some time.

> *"I overheard a conversation the other day between two col-leagues: one said to the other, 'You're defining yourself by your job title, not defining the job by who you are'."*
> ANDREW JACOBS, LEARNING AND DEVELOPMENT MANAGER.

Many people also go through life describing themselves as 'just a . . .', be it 'housewife', 'salesman', 'civil servant', 'teacher', 'banker' or whatever.

This suggests two problems:

- getting tied up with a 'job title';
- belittling your abilities internally so they appear less to others.

It is important to really analyse all the things that you *can do*, rather than the things that you have already achieved. For instance:

Think of one unassuming chap named Earnest Shackleton: he took part in an expedition to the Antarctic but had to retire sick. He then tried to become the first man to reach the South Pole. He failed. He then tried to cross Antarctica via the Pole, but failed again. He went back for a third time but died of a heart attack. He died heavily in debt and never achieved any of his major goals in life.

Not a very successful chap?

Well, he did get knighted, made a Commander of the Royal Victorian Order, awarded an OBE and, perhaps most important, his staff would (and did literally) follow him to the ends of the earth. He is also credited as one of the greatest leaders the human race has ever produced. What he could do was almost endless, what he achieved in terms of tangible 'success' was rather less.

Make a list of all the things that you have done and/or do. Include the things that you do or did at school, college, university, any part-time or full-time jobs you may have had, any unpaid volunteering you did or do, anything you do for family and neighbours, or if you are a parent anything that you do for the children. If you are a homeowner, include the things you do around the home and garden.

This may seem as if you are scraping the proverbial barrel, but what you are actually doing is looking at your 'transferable skills' in order to raise your self-esteem and open up your options.

If you consider, for example, running the home and being a parent (single or married) you might on any average day, do the following things:

- get self up;
- get the children up;
- feed and dress them;
- get them off to school;
- do the grocery shopping;
- do a Zumba class;
- pay some bills;
- fill in the child allowance forms;
- tidy and clean the house;
- pick the children up from school;
- entertain them for a while;
- get them to do their homework;
- feed them their supper;
- put them to bed.

Now break down each of the things you do into the requisite skills, knowledge or characteristics that you possess or demonstrate in order to do them as well as you do.

Use a simple two-column table like this:

Task	Skills, knowledge, characteristics
■ Get self up	Self-motivated, aware of deadlines, takes responsibility
■ Get the children up	Able to motivate others successfully
■ Feed and dress them	Able to plan and organise
■ Get them off to school	Driver, safety-aware
■ Do the grocery shopping	Manages budgets, plans and coordinates
■ Do a Zumba class	Social skills, healthy, committed
■ Pay some bills	Numerate, aware of/keeps to deadlines
■ Fill in the child allowance forms	Literate, able to understand bureaucracy
■ Tidy and clean the house	Quality/attention to detail

You will quickly find that actually you have quite a long list of skills, knowledge and personal characteristics that will make you feel quite good about yourself; they may also start to point you in the direction of a particular career.

Another proven way to increase self-esteem for many people is the concept of helping others. You don't have to be the 'Secret Millionaire' or head up a not-for-profit organisation to raise your self-esteem by helping others; 'random acts of kindness' generally work just as well. Make an effort to identify opportunities to exhibit these little, low-cost, high-impact actions:

- holding a door open for someone;
- getting something down from a high shelf for someone;
- helping a mum with a pushchair up the steps;
- picking up a piece of casually discarded litter;
- offering someone your seat on the tube or the bus;
- offering to do something for a neighbour.

It is also worth bearing in mind that happiness and self-esteem are usually linked and therefore you can raise your self-esteem by finding ways to raise your levels of happiness. Back in Chapter 4 there was a 'Read it and reap activity' around the book *Thank You* by Liggy Webb (see page 66). Remember to say thank you for other people's random acts of kindness; surprisingly, it does also make you feel better about yourself.

In much the same way that there is a direct link between your physical health and the psychological condition of stress, there is a clear link for many people between their physical appearance and their feeling of self-esteem and therefore confidence:

- Soldiers fight more effectively when they know that they look warlike (this covers their clothes, camouflage face-paint and their equipment).
- Con artists are more able to act their role when they feel appropriately dressed and equipped.
- Many down-and-outs suddenly exude spirit and confidence after a bath, a shave, a haircut and a set of clean clothes.

For some long-term unemployed people the simple fact that they are out of the habit of being dressed in 'business clothes' (which may be a suit or overalls) has a debilitating effect on their belief that they can and will get back into work. And this is before you start taking into account other people's view of whether you look like a successful businessman or an out-of-work student (see the possibly apocryphal story in Chapter 5 concerning Richard Branson, on page 70.)

'Dress for Success' is a not-for-profit organisation that recognises the importance of appearance, not just on the recruitment interviewer but also on the confidence and self-esteem of the interviewee. Since 1997 they have provided appropriate business clothing and grooming advice to over half-a-million people worldwide to help them to not only *get* jobs, but also to *keep* them; in other words not just to con an interviewer but to raise the self-esteem of the individual to a point where they can maintain a higher level of performance.

In Chapter 5 we looked at your *image* and the effect it had on other people; now take a look at yourself in the mirror, and ask yourself: 'What effect does my reflection have on *me*?'

- What effect does my grooming, shaving (designer stubble or too-hungover-to-care), hair (cleanliness, length, style, condition), nails (bitten, manicured, polished), make-up, jewellery, spectacles, teeth (not Hollywood gleam caps and crowns but clean and not punctuated by bits of last night's supper) have on me? Do I look as if I care about my everyday appearance or have I given up (or some-where in between)?

- What about the *coordination* of my clothes? Do I look as if I made a conscious effort to match tops and bottoms or just put on the first things that came to hand that weren't too dirty?

- What about the *condition* of my clothes? Do I look as if I make an effort here or are they torn, worn, buttons missing, ill-fitting?

No one is suggesting that you have to go and buy a whole lot of high-fashion or even high-quality clothing in order to boost your self-esteem; but most people do report that knowing that they look smart and clean and cared-for *does* boost their self-esteem, even if their clothes are old or unfashionable or even the same as everyone else around you.

It is hard to have much self-esteem if you are permanently exhausted, so here are two potentially helpful sets of tips. First, thirteen things to do if you are feeling tired to try to give yourself a bit of oomph. And second, nine ways to avoid getting tired, thus allowing you to find the energy to boost your self-esteem by doing things you might otherwise be too tired to do.

How to stay awake and alert when you are tired

1 Get moving. The more oxygen that runs through you, the more energised you'll feel. *Walking* – even if it's just around the block or to the other end of the building – is one way to feel alert and energised. The more physically active you are, the less fatigue you'll feel. Exercise releases hormones that make you feel alive, refreshed and energised all day. *Jump/jog on the spot quietly . . .*

jump something high (like an imaginary skipping rope) and quickly, but try to land quietly . . . this will help wake up your muscles with movement and oxygen and allow you a bit more control to prevent injuries.

2 Reduce fatigue with dark chocolate! People who consume moderate amounts of dark chocolate have better brain circulation. Cocoa beans – the main ingredient in chocolate – contain natural antioxidants called cocoa flavonoids. The flavonoids in chocolate are also more powerful than vitamin C at limiting fatty deposits (plaque) in arteries in the brain and heart. Build-ups of plaque can impair mental performance. Have two small squares of a bar of chocolate. The darker the chocolate, the better. According to the ORAC scale – a measure of the antioxidant levels in foods – dark chocolate has double the amount of antioxidants of milk chocolate.

3 Splash cold water on the pulse area of your wrists.

4 Expose yourself to bright light, preferably natural daylight. Your body's internal clock, its circadian rhythms, are regulated by your exposure to sufficient light. Even if you're in an environment where there's artificial light, brighter is better. If you can step outside (even on a cloudy day) or look out of the window for a full minute, you'll be more alert. Wherever you are, see if you can upgrade the light bulb or add a lamp that will brighten your workspace.

5 Make fists with your feet; this is a recommended method for overcoming jet lag (it was featured in the original *Die Hard* movie!) Slip your shoes off and bunch your toes, bend your ankles back as far as you can and roll your feet around holding the bunching; do this for a minute or so.

6 Use your sense of smell. A strong scent, good or bad, can make you more alert very quickly; think 'smelling salts'! Holistic healthcare providers often recommend essential oils of the following plants to stimulate the nervous system and reduce fatigue (open the bottle and take a big whiff when you're feeling drowsy):

- rosemary;

- eucalyptus blue gum;

- peppermint (a study showed that smelling peppermint can lower fatigue by 15 per cent, increase alertness by 30 per cent and decrease frustration by 25 per cent);

- Scots pine oil.

Of course, not all of us have essential oils to hand, but using hand lotions, scent or aftershave can help. The smell of coffee also works (beans or brewed, study has shown that simply smelling coffee can awaken a person.) A Vicks inhaler or Olbas Oil works for some people and is a pocketable commodity.

7 Use acupressure. Massaging any of the following points will improve circulation and ease fatigue:

- top of your head (lightly tap with your fingertip);

- top of the back of your neck;

- back of your hands (between thumb and index finger);

- just below the knees;

- earlobes.

8 Don't forget that a little caffeine can help a lot. *Making* a cup of tea or coffee will *get you up and moving* and provide some caffeine to perk you up as well.

9 Listen to music that you personally find energising; music that you find irritating or jarring can also work.

10 Eat an apple – the sweetness and tartness in the flavour, along with the 'crunch', will perk you up in a healthy way.

11 Drink a glass of ice cold water (the coldness picks you up, and guarantees you getting up every half hour or so to go to the loo; you won't nod off with a full bladder).

12 Brush your teeth.

How to avoid getting tired

Check for other medical problems. Tiredness is a common symptom of thyroid problems, depression, chronic fatigue syndrome and other medical problems. If you've been fighting tiredness for weeks, see your doctor. It's better to rule out other possible medical conditions than fight tiredness in vain.

1 Vary your routine. A great way to avoid fatigue is to do something different. Change the route you take to work, start a different hobby, take an evening class, meet new people – those are activities that could help you feel energised about life in general. Never underestimate the power of positive mental attitude.

2 Avoid simple carbohydrates. The sugar in soft drinks, chips, rice, crisps, chocolate and anything white and processed causes your blood sugar levels to spike. You are fighting fatigue by eating sugar, but only short-term; your body then releases insulin, which makes you feel tired.

3 Eat complex carbohydrates. Food that breaks down slowly will help you feel energised all day. Healthy muesli bars, bagels and pasta are complex carbohydrates that release energy slowly, which helps fight fatigue.

4 Check your iron levels; a simple way to feel alert is to make sure you're getting enough iron. Eat fish, eggs, chicken, fortified cereals and beans to fight fatigue.

5 Stay at a healthy weight. You don't have to be slim to be healthy and fit. In fact, if you're too slim you'll feel tired, drained and listless. And if you're overweight, you'll get tired when you climb a flight of stairs. To stay energised all day, maintain a healthy weight.

6 Maintain your weight sensibly. To fight fatigue, don't go to extremes (skipping meals or over-exercising). Eat those complex carbohydrates every two or three hours, and stop eating before you're full.

7 Go to bed at the same time every night. Studies show that the time you go to bed is more important than the time you get up.

8 Even though drinking coffee is a suggested 'band aid' method, this is just a temporary fix. As soon as the caffeine wears off you are back to point a. And this is when the vicious cycle begins. After the first cup wears off you go back and get another, and then after that another. This is not a safe way to fight fatigue, and if this sounds familiar you should definitely try an alternative option.

9 Take a holiday. This is one of the best ways to fight fatigue at work. If you feel like you cannot catch up, the best thing to do is take some time off. Even if you do nothing more than lie around the house, you will still be giving your mind a rest from work. But do not forget that a holiday means no work: don't take work on holiday, don't pick up emails – delegate and relax.

SOME FINAL REFLECTIONS ON THE SUBJECT OF SELF-ESTEEM

"When we see people acting in an abusive, arrogant, or demeaning manner toward others, their behaviour almost always is a symptom of their lack of self-esteem. They need to put someone else down to feel good about themselves." CLAYTON M. CHRISTENSEN, HARVARD BUSINESS SCHOOL.

Or, more pithily . . .

"No one can make you feel inferior without your consent." ELEANOR ROOSEVELT, US FIRST LADY 1933–1945.

"I pity the fool who has to put down others to build up his own self-esteem." MR T., *THE A TEAM*.

Think about these quotations: what they mean to you about your own self-esteem, and what and how you maintain it at a level that keeps you happy and healthy but doesn't damage anyone with whom you come into contact.

CHAPTER 10

Putting it back

WHY BOTHER BEING ALTRUISTIC?

You may find the premise of this chapter a bit weird; the book is about your career, but this chapter is about going out into society and doing things for nothing. Surely that is going to distract you from your career isn't it?

Well, maybe not. Doing things for altruistic reasons can, and often does, have many more tangible benefits, as I have found myself.

CASE STUDY

In 2007 I offered to design and deliver some training for a small local charity as a freebie. As I wrote the training material it blossomed into a 60-page detailed 'manual' on the subject.

In 2008 I offered the 60-page manual to a start-up organisation that was building an online resource for managers; the offer was to provide it free with a view to receiving a possible royalty later on, when the website started to make a profit.

In 2009, as a result of someone seeing my work on the website, I was asked if I'd like to 'tender' to write a book in a series being commissioned by a major UK publisher. I did, and got the contract to write two titles. Shortly before the deadline another author fell ill, and as I had already finished my work the publisher asked if I could write a third book, in double-quick time.

In 2010 the website broke into profit and I got my first royalty cheque from the website owner.

Later in 2010 I was offered the chance to write another book by a different client, based on the three I wrote in 2009.

Then in 2011 I successfully pitched an idea to another major publishing house and was commissioned to write a new book, which you are reading right now!

ASK NOT WHAT SOCIETY CAN DO FOR YOU, BUT WHAT YOU CAN DO FOR SOCIETY!

Not everyone has the wherewithal to write a book or to provide the sort of assistance to a charity that I did, but pretty much every charity and not-for-profit organisation (NFP) in the world welcomes the support and assistance of volunteers, regardless of whether they provide no more than a pair of free hands or highly specialised intellectual knowledge. Most not-for-profit organisations are also happy to receive help for a couple of hours a quarter, or a couple of hours a week – what you are able to give is almost always gratefully received.

Consider what you could offer to a not-for-profit organisation: this could be a registered charity, or social enterprises, parish councils, pressure groups, residents' associations, 'friends of' groups, religious groups/congregations, movements such as the Guides or Scouts, or even official organisations such as the Special Constabulary, the TA, RNVR, RAFVR, RNLI or mountain/cave rescue. We might even be looking at amateur dramatics groups, choirs or bands.

- Could you offer labour? Most heritage-type NFPs require a consistent supply of unskilled labour to do tasks ranging from clearing undergrowth to digging out overgrown canals, from painting walls to cleaning off graffiti, from picking up litter to directing traffic in a car park.

- Could you offer an artisanal skill? Again, many heritage-type NFPs require the services of skilled people to repair tapestries, carve stone and wood, lay bricks and similar.

- Could you provide your technical skill and equipment to a needy NFP? A vehicle and driver for 'meals-on-wheels', a piece of plant and an operator to dig a pond, a generator and lighting set for the Grand Ball, a marquee.

- Could you provide 'office administration' type services? Most NFPs have a need for typing, filing, archiving, phone answering and bookkeeping people.

- Could you provide a 'professional' skill? Most NFPs have either a consistent or an occasional need for accountants, publicists, surveyors, curators, lawyers, architects and auctioneers.

- Could you provide a fundraising input? This can be any-thing from selling poppies for Remembrance Day, through to drafting requests for corporate sponsorships and dona-tions, or, if you happen to have a particular relevant skill such as singing, providing the entertainment at fundraisers.

- Could you offer your personality/life experience/ears? Many of the NFPs that aim to help disadvantaged or suf-fering people have a need for coaches, mentors and people prepared to act as a sounding board or just a shoulder to cry on.

- Could you lend your name? If you happen to be famous, most NFPs need patrons.

OK, *NOW* ASK WHAT SOCIETY CAN DO FOR YOU!

Now consider what an NFP *could offer you*.

- The boost to your self-esteem that you get from doing something 'good'.

- New skills: many NFPs provide (or insist on) formal train-ing and development opportunities for their volunteers for gratis. These can range from health and safety training through to specialist training relevant to the organisation (the Citizens' Advice Bureau provide excellent training for all their advisors.) You also learn 'on the job', often from experienced and highly skilled people.

- A new circle of friends and acquaintances in your fellow volunteers, the employed staff of the NFP and possibly the clients/beneficiaries.

- A sense of purpose outside your day job.

- A change of scenery from your day job. (If you are an accountant who seldom gets out of the office between Monday and Friday, what better way to spend half of Saturday than working on clearing undergrowth on the canal banks with a bill hook and a workboat?)

- A change of responsibility from your day job (in the week you are a captain of industry but at the weekend you are a labourer with no worries and someone else to take the lead.)

- Respect in the community.

- The chance to be the first to know about things that may affect your locality . . . or the chance to have your say in these things, before others do. (This is why a lot of people join their parish council!)

- The opportunity to be in the running for an MBE!

Having read the two lists above, think about:

a) what you might have to offer;

b) what you might enjoy (doing your 'civic' duty should be fun, not a pain!); and

c) what you hope to get out of it (there is a big philosophical debate about whether there is a such a thing as a truly selfless act.)

CALL TO ACTION!

Now use a search engine to find out what local (or online) organisations exist that may be looking for volunteers. Most UK towns have some sort of 'clearing house' that acts as a focal point for volunteers to make contact with organisations seeking volunteers; these are often styled as 'Voluntary Action' groups. Alternatively, search 'charities in *your town*'.

Many professions have a 'pro bono' organisation, which may be run by the professional association itself (as in the case of surveyors – the RICS), or by members of the profession via Facebook/LinkedIn, or as a stand-alone organisation, such as Charity Days.

If you don't want to offer your time, effort and/or expertise *via a non-profit organisation*, you can always simply try to engage in 'random acts of kindness':

1 Send someone who deserves it a handwritten note of thanks.

2 If you are cutting your hedge or lawn, offer to cut your neighbour's hedge or lawn.

3 Give a compliment *about* your waiter/waitress *to* their manager.

4 Stop and offer to help someone who is broken down.

5 Let someone jump in front of you in a queue if they look like they need to.

6 Hold the door open for someone.

7 Tell someone if their car's lights aren't working.

8 Make a coffee/tea for someone who is working hard.

9 Post an online complimentary review of a product, book or venue that deserves it.

10 Say 'thank you' to anyone who holds a door open for you!

11 Say 'thank you' to the bus driver/train conductor/check-out operator.

12 Give up your seat for someone who looks as if they need it more than you do.

13 Pick up some rubbish in the road that would otherwise be lying around.

14 Compliment someone.

15 Go and say 'thank you' to someone who does a 'thankless task' – street-sweepers, dustmen, store security guards, 'Johnny-no-stars' wiping the tables in the take-away, even a traffic warden (you never know, your being nice to them could just make them deal more patiently with the next person who feels unfairly penalised by a ticket.)

16 Recommend a competitor to a potential client.

17 Give another driver your parking spot.

18 Call on an elderly/housebound neighbour and spend a bit of time with them . . .

19 . . . let them know when you are popping to the shops so you can pick up something they need.

20 Phone a family member who doesn't live with you.

21 Leave a copy of an interesting book on a train/bus.

22 Send a thank you note to a person who has helped you in the past, even if it is years since they helped you.

23 Smile . . . a lot.

24 Take a quick look through your wardrobe and donate something to a charity shop that you haven't worn for six months.

25 Let the person behind you in the checkout queue have your Nectar points/whatever-for-schools-vouchers if you don't need them.

26 Be nice to the person who rings you just as you are sitting down to dinner to try to sell you solar panels/life insurance/double glazing/a lifestyle survey (you don't have to buy anything, just be 'nice'). You can even ask them, *nicely*, to take you off their contact list.

27 Put a couple of pennies in every charity box you see.

28 Offer to do a little chore for your partner that they usually have to do.

29 Share your umbrella with someone who is getting wet.

30 Help someone up the steps with their shopping trolley, baby-buggy or luggage.

CHAPTER 11

Learning and earning

THE 'I-DIDN'T-GET-WHERE-I-AM-TODAY . . .' TRAP

"Smart people don't learn . . . because they have too much invested in proving what they know and avoiding being seen as not knowing." PROFESSOR CHRIS ARGYRIS, HARVARD BUSINESS SCHOOL.

In many people's minds, the concept that they still have things to learn is a sign of weakness – a suggestion that if they don't already know everything they cannot be worthy of their current role.

Frankly, this is tosh!

CASE STUDY

In the mid 1990s a senior executive, Tom Roberts, was having trouble with his computer. The technical guy from the IT department came to look at the machine and discovered that several of the keys were stuck down with a brown sticky deposit. It turned out to be hot chocolate. Tom had put his cup into 'the cup-holder' in the PC tower and it had spilled.

That, however, isn't the point of the story. The technical support guy explained what the CD-ROM drive actually was and how it worked and asked Tom why he was unaware of the whole matter. Tom replied that someone had made his secretary redundant and replaced her with a desktop computer, but no one had trained him to use it and, since he was a highly paid executive, he hadn't felt it appropriate to openly admit that he couldn't understand what a 17-year-old school-leaver could understand. So he simply didn't use the computer for anything he couldn't already do.

The tech support guy happened to mention this to a friend who was from the HR department. The company instigated a 'Training-Needs Amnesty' for all senior managers to privately and quietly get brought up to speed with anything they needed to learn.

In her book, *Nine Things Successful People Do Differently*, Heidi Halvorson notes that one ingredient of success is the focus on 'getting better' rather than on 'being good'. She claims that many people seem to believe that their intelligence, personality and physical aptitudes are immovable – that no matter what they do, they won't and can't improve. Consequently, they focus on what they can achieve *now*, rather than what they could achieve if they first developed themselves by acquiring new knowledge and skills.

In reality, this belief in fixed ability is completely wrong; while each of us may have certain natural aptitudes we can all get better at virtually anything, we can improve ourselves and develop new knowledge, skills and abilities. People who set themselves goals to improve, take difficulty in their stride. And they tend to appreciate the journey as much as the destination.

"Learning is not compulsory . . . neither is survival." DR W. EDWARDS DEMING, AUTHOR, PROFESSOR, CONSULTANT AND FATHER OF JAPAN'S POST-WAR INDUSTRIAL RECOVERY.

YOU DON'T HAVE TO BE BAD TO GET BETTER

The reality is that we *can* all learn (and we all *do* learn) every day, although there are some people who follow the theory of these great thinkers:

"How is education supposed to make me feel smarter? Besides, every time I learn something new, it pushes some old stuff out of my brain." HOMER SIMPSON.

"I cannot do with any more education, Jeeves. I was full up years ago!" BERTIE WOOSTER.

But more sensible folk prefer to follow the lead of Mahatma Gandhi:

Live as if you were to die tomorrow. Learn as if you were to live forever.

We can learn intuitively or we can learn intentionally.

When we learn *intuitively* we learn simply by our normal everyday actions, we learn from our experience – our mistakes and successes and the mistakes and successes of others that we see or hear about. We learn by reading the paper, watching the television, by talking to others.

What we don't often do is to notice formally that we are learning, and by this omission we often have to repeat the lesson several times before the learning actually clicks in and changes our behaviour.

We can learn *intentionally* in two ways: through experience and through new exposure.

To learn intentionally through experience we follow the same path as intuitive learning, but we stop after each experience and reflect on what we have learned and how and where it may help us. For example, imagine that you, as a young fresh recruit, have just been to a meeting with your boss and several other members of the team. In your judgement, the meeting was a severe waste of your time; you had to listen to some other people debating at length on a topic that was completely outside your sphere of interest and even then they didn't actually get any decisions made. On the topics that were of relevance to you your boss did listen to your opinion, and the opinion of others, and a couple of decisions were sort of made. But the decisions were of the 'we will' variety and you came out of the meeting unsure of whether you were waiting for a colleague to do something or whether they were reliant on you doing it. Neither of you has any idea *when* it has to be done by.

Let us reflect on what we have learned:

■ It is not always necessary for everyone to attend a whole meeting if large parts of the meeting are to discuss and decide on things that don't affect them.

- It is a good idea in any meeting to agree beforehand whether there is a need simply to discuss a topic or whether it is necessary to make decisions. If decisions need to be made this should be done in the meeting and recorded.

- It is important that responsibilities and action plans are allocated at the end of discussions to ensure that people know what is expected of them next.

Let us reflect on how and where this may help you:

- It may help you next time your boss schedules a meeting; you may be able to agree to attend only part of the meeting, or to hold a separate meeting that is relevant only to you.

- It may help you in meetings to ensure that you ask the right questions to get the information you need to make you more efficient.

- It may help you when you start chairing meetings to avoid the errors your boss is making/allowing to be made that make their meetings so unproductive!

We can also learn intentionally from new exposure; in this instance we deliberately expose ourselves to new knowledge or skill with the deliberate intent of learning from it. We can do this by an increasing variety of different methods:

a) Read a book on the subject: even with the demise of the lending library and the ability to browse the shelves, online bookstores (with their search facilities and the capacity to show what others who looked at a particular title also viewed) are an excellent place for discovering what is in print about pretty much any topic under the sun.

b) Visit a website: the internet is a free and virtually unre-stricted resource. There are special-interest websites on such a wide variety of topics that it is almost impossible to get bored online (and which is why the internet can also be such a destructive force!) Many websites have free down-loadable resources, 'white papers', PDFs and podcasts, as well as the main text of the site.

c) Subscribe to a special-interest magazine (real or increas-ingly virtual); there are newsletters, blogs and features being released daily.

d) 'Follow' appropriate tweeters on Twitter: yes, there is an awful lot of drivel included in those 147-character mes-sages, but there is a lot of interesting and potentially useful information as well.

e) 'Take a class': again you can do this in the real world at your local adult education centre:

Just looking at my local college, they run 138 part-time and evening adult education courses (not including 'essen-tial skills' of Mathematics and English) that range from Wiring Regulations through Accounting, Photography, Sign Language, Computer Programming, Welding, Marketing, Human Resource Management, First Aid, Hospitality Management, Counselling, Teaching, Hairdressing, Fitness Instructing to Website Design.

Or you can do it virtually by either buying (or getting a free download of) an e-learning program, or you can sign up to a free live webinar and learn from the comfort of your own home. Consider visiting **http://www.collegeathome. com/blog/2008/06/17/learn-anything-100-places-to-find-free-webinars-and-tutorials/** where you will find a vast array of links to places where you can get free online material for learning.

Or you can . . .

f) . . . 'go back to school'.

CASE STUDY

Anita Terry had not done very well in school and had left as soon as possible and joined the Navy. Sadly, she was soon diagnosed as being partially deaf and was discharged on medical grounds. She married and had a child but her husband left her when their son was just a toddler. Her ex was not good at making maintenance payments.

She moved into social housing and got a part-time job as a classroom assistant at the primary school in which she had enrolled her son.

After a year she decided that she liked teaching and that she had a natural aptitude. She enrolled at the Open University to study for a degree. She worked hard at the school, and at being a (single) Mum and at her studies.

As soon as she qualified she signed up for a master's degree. She still worked hard as a junior teacher, her son gave her all the parental headaches that children are wont to give their parents, and she carried on studying.

When she got her master's she became the best qualified person in the staffroom, but there was no vacancy in the school for a fully fledged teacher. So she moved to another, larger school in the area.

Within 10 years she became the head teacher of a not-insubstantial primary school, complete with a significant salary and benefits package, and, most importantly, she was very happy.

The wonderful thing is that the phrase 'go back to school' is itself dreadfully outdated. Yes, if you can afford it you can take the full-time educational route but, as Bill Gates pointed out at the Techonomy Conference on the 6 August 2010:

Place-based colleges are good for parties, but are becoming less crucial for learning thanks to the internet.

The Open University has been in business in the UK since January 1971, offering 'proper' academic qualifications (rather than just courses), and many other universities now offer part-time routes to academic and professional qualifications.

g) Find a mentor or mentors: most people are deeply touched to be considered an expert in their chosen field, so if you want to learn something and you can find someone who seems to be something of a guru in the subject, ask them to tell/show/teach you. This is particularly good for their self-esteem! Don't be fooled by the 'wise old owl' image of a mentor – you can often learn something from someone less than half your age; and we are not only talking about how to programme the satellite TV!

"If your attitude is that only smarter people have something to teach you, your learning opportunities will be very limited. But if you have a humble eagerness to learn something from everybody, your learning opportunities will be unlimited." CLAYTON M. CHRISTENSEN, HARVARD BUSINESS SCHOOL.

There are also 'communities of practice' all over the internet, where people post ad hoc learning needs, 'How do I . . .?', and people with expertise in the subject respond and share their knowledge. Many of these are services where you need to register, but most are free and in most cases you can even create a user-name that is an alias so you don't leave a trail of ignorance across cyberspace.

h) Barter some learning in return for your time: find a voluntary position where you can get some relevant training or supervised experience (see Chapter 9 for more details).

j) Step outside your comfort zone/throw yourself in at the deep end: just go and try something that you have never done before. Within reason, this is a great way to learn from experience, whether you are doing it at work and volunteering to take on something new (to you) or whether you are doing it at home and trying a new recipe or DIY project. Yes, you will often find out that there was a lot that you didn't know that you didn't know but, so long as you aren't trying something potentially dangerous (like fitting a new gas cooker or making an omelette out of some unidentified mushrooms that you found on a walk), it is a wonderful voyage of discovery. Not only will you learn a new skill but you will learn something about yourself, and other people may learn something about you as well.

"I am always doing that which I cannot do, in order that I may learn how to do it." PABLO PICASSO, PAINTER & SCULPTOR

THE ULTIMATE REASON TO LEARN – FOR THE LOVE OF LEARNING RATHER THAN FINANCIAL GAIN

You don't have to learn something solely for the purpose of furthering your career; you may also decide to learn a new knowledge or skill:

- to save money: DIY, car maintenance, dressmaking;
- to express your creativity: dressmaking, painting, sculpture, photography, cookery;
- to improve the lot of your family: cookery, budgeting;
- to improve your physical or psychological health: Tai Chi, Yoga, Zumba, cookery, golf, meditation, anger management;
- to improve your holidays: a language or foreign culture.

CASE STUDY

A London couple used to book their holiday each year to a different country and then spend the time before they went learning the language, either via their local adult education centre or by using a home-study course. By the time they reached retirement age they could both identify and speak, to a 'tourist' level, nine different languages. In retirement they 'worked' as troubleshooters for their local tourist information centre and the police, helping out when visitors to the UK ran into problems.

- to improve your spare time/just to learn for the sake of learning: the University of the Third Age (U3A) is an organisation that provides activities and learning for people over the age of 50. It is a relatively informal organisation, with lectures and meetings on subjects ranging from Mah Jong to digital photography, Russian to military history.

Take time to consider what *you* would like to learn:

- for your current career – technical or managerial skills or knowledge;
- for a future career or career change;
- to save you money or make you a more rounded person;
- for your personal improvement or your health;
- for the sheer joy of learning something.

> *"Personally, I am always ready to learn, although I do not always like being taught."* WINSTON CHURCHILL, FORMER PRIME MINISTER

Take time to consider *how* you would like to learn:

- totally self-managed – via reading, internet searching and study;
- self-paced but formal learning – distance learning, e-learning course, find a mentor;
- tutor-led – via some sort of volunteering;
- tutor-led – via the local adult education provider;

- tutor-led and leading to a paper qualification – via a college, university or institute;
- 'experiential' – by trying it out.

Linked to this, consider *when and where* you would like to learn:

- during the working day;
- during the evenings;
- at weekends;
- at work;
- at home;
- at a college/university or institute;
- or even . . .

CASE STUDY

Phil Bennison spent an hour and a half each morning and evening sitting on a train commuting to and from work. He wanted to get a professional qualification and institute membership in the discipline he had chosen for his career. He enrolled in a correspondence course with a reputable provider and spent his travelling time reading the required texts and planning his essays and project submissions. He wrote the essays during his lunch breaks at his desk at work.

After three years he sat his final exams on one day, which he took as holiday. Five weeks later he was formally able to add the post-nominal letters for Chartered Membership of the Institute after his name.

His 2,400 hours of study were completed predominantly during the otherwise brain-dead time of sitting on a commuter train.

Take time to consider how you will *fund* this learning:

- Will you ask your employer to pay for it?

  If you go down this route, be aware that it is only reasonable that the employer see a return on their investment; i.e. that you commit to a certain length of service after completion or that you agree to a payback schedule in the event that you leave the organisation.

- Will you try to find it for free?

- Will you barter for it with your time by volunteering?

- Will you seek government/charity funding?

  See **http://www.direct.gov.uk/en/EducationAnd Learning/AdultLearning/FinancialHelpForAdult Learners/DG_10033132** for details, or search through the Educational Grants Directory (published by the Directory of Social Change), the Charities Digest (Waterlow Information Services), The Grants Register (Macmillan Press) and The Directory of Grant Making Trusts (Charities Aid Foundation).

■ Will you pay for it yourself?

Most providers have finance schemes available, but do ensure that you read the small print before you sign up.

Once you have answered these questions then get out and start learning!

CHAPTER 12

Getting the word out there

Although this book is more about 'career coaching' than 'job search', there are two elements that we will look at here:

- publicising your image; and
- networking.

YOUR PR

In Chapter 5 you looked at your image and what you want the world to see you as; in this section we look in greater detail at how you are going to actually get that image within eyeshot of the *appropriate* public.

What constitutes an *appropriate* public will depend on what you have decided to do. For instance, if you are planning on politics as a career then the relevant electorate (local or national or party membership) is the appropriate public. If you are looking at a career in, say, the motor trade, then motor dealership management and the specialist recruitment industry may be the appropriate public. If you are intending to pursue a career (permanently or for a given period) as a homemaker, then other local homemakers are the appropriate public.

The important thing is to actively identify the demographic of people who will be able to help or hinder you and then actively plan how you are going to get the image to them.

CASE STUDY

Paul had completed his professional training and started his first job in a rather staid and hidebound organisation. Not wanting to simply trust to others for his promotional opportunities, he planned a concerted campaign to get himself noticed by the right people for the right reasons.

Every eight days he hand-delivered a very brief 'report' to a member of the executive team, ensuring that each person was targeted at least once every seven weeks. His report always offered a suggested improvement for some aspect of that manager's department. He was careful to couch the suggestions in such a way that they never appeared critical of current working practice or staff, but always offered an idea for becoming even better.

Within a year this young graduate had raised a positive profile with every single member of the executive board. It's unsurprising, then, that when a special project came up his name was the first in virtually all their minds as a go-getting young thinker who obviously relished a challenge. His PR campaign was entirely successful and his promotion came very early.

Back in Chapter 5 you looked at your current virtual presence:

- LinkedIn: are you? Is it up to date? What does it say about you?
- Facebook: does this portray the image you want?
- Friends Reunited: as above;
- Twitter: do you tweet? If so what?
- any other social networking sites;
- your own website, 'vanity' or corporate;
- your voicemail greeting on your work and private and mobile phones: your own voice? Short and sweet or rambling?
- any special interest forum to which you may belong;
- your employer's website;
- any press/media mentions of you.

Now what you need to do is to take this a stage further and decide whether you need to manage an active PR campaign using these media and any others that are appropriate to your career aims.

Think about the following questions to get you going:

1 **Who is your target audience?** Are they potential employers/customers (e.g. senior managers or parents), or influencers of potential employers/customers (e.g. PAs to senior managers, or children)?

2 **'Where' are they?** Are they geographically clustered, in a specific industry sector or demographic? Where do they

'cluster'? For instance, directors of medium-sized and larger organisations may cluster at the Institute of Directors (the IoD), whereas directors of small businesses may cluster at their local Rotary club or Chamber of Commerce.

3 **What are appropriate media to use to get your message across to them?** For instance, if they are in-house (as in the case study above) an email may be appropriate; if they are at the IoD or Chamber of Commerce, then an offer to present at a meeting may be better; if they are spread across the land/globe, then an email newsletter may be appropriate.

4 **Is the medium outside your *control*?** (You control whether you send an email but you cannot control whether a trade magazine will publish an article that you write.) What can you do to increase the likelihood of success? Well, you could spend some time building a good relationship with the features editor of the magazine so that the next time they are looking for someone to quote or to write an article, you will be at the top of their mind as a useful contact.

5 **What are the timeframes?** When should you start? How long should you go on? How often should you 'touch' your market? Many people and organisations send out newsletters almost daily – they frequently become the electronic version of junk mail and most people just don't bother to read them. Paradoxically, they can become an annoyance and can actually have the opposite effect to the desired one.

6 **What do you 'give' people?** What ISTATOYs (**I S**aw **T**his **A**nd **T**hought **O**f **Y**ou) can you give people? These should be things that are relevant, pertinent, appropriate and/or of

value to the recipient. Yes, you can give ISTATOYs that are material items that you know the recipient will value, but this can become costly and can show little or no return on investment. Companies also have rules about their staff accepting 'gifts', which can be seen as bribes. The best ISTATOYs are often knowledge or ideas: snippets of helpful information or tips, suggestions or recommendations. Whether you Tweet a tiny URL to someone else's useful article or whether you send your own 'white paper' will depend on the circumstance. Generally speaking, though, jokes, funny pictures and the like are not really ISTATOYs.

7 **Are there any 'affiliates' that you can associate with in order to upgrade the credibility of your PR campaign?** For instance, would getting an article published in the *Harvard Business Review* stand you in better stead than publishing on eZine.com, or would Mumsnet be better for your needs?

8 Are there any 'tricks' that you can use to differentiate your approach from everyone else's?

CASE STUDIES

Alana wanted to work in a very sought-after organisation and she knew that the manager there received lots of unsolicited mail, most of which just got shredded. So she shredded the bottom 3cm of her letter to the manager, explaining in the first paragraph that it would probably be junked so she was helping the manager out.

She got asked to a meeting in under 24 hours.

Christine wanted to get into the creative side of advertising; she burned her opening letter onto a piece of driftwood with a pyrography set and mailed it parcel post. They gave her a project within a week of its receipt.

A planned approach to your PR is going to be far more effective than a piecemeal and ad hoc approach, so after you have considered these questions sit down and make a plan, then stick to it!

NETWORKING

We introduced networking in Chapter 3, but that was for the purpose of finding out about possible careers; now you need to start thinking about networking as a way of getting your name out to as many people as possible who could help you to actually get paid work. There are two potential starting points:

1 You are at the start of your career or are planning on making a new career or life in a new region or country.

2 You are already in your chosen career but are just beginning to get serious about pushing yourself forward and trying to get the most out of it.

Both scenarios begin in very similar ways but from different places. Let's look at the career-starters in group 1 first.

Much as you did back in Chapter 3, you start off with all the people you know already; you never know who these people know or where they have friends and relatives.

Now you start with a sensible approach to the chosen area:

- Identify any appropriate trade associations, unions, professional groups or networking clubs that are available in the career sector or geographical region in which you are interested. You can find them via an internet search – for example, searching 'networking clubs in Hampshire' produces over 1 million results. Frankly, most of these results are of little use, but just a couple of minutes spent on it shows nine active networking clubs in the first few pages, including a networking club of American Expats in Hampshire. Similar results are gained by searching for 'professional groups in Singapore' and 'trade associations in Yorkshire'. You can also search in the industry area – for example, 'professional groups in the motor trade' will get everything from the Independent Automotive Professionals Association to the Scottish Motor Trade Association.

- Having identified appropriate associations, go along to some of their meetings and introduce yourself to as many people as you can, and talk to them. See what the format of their meetings is, hand out some of those calling cards, mentioned in Chapter 8, and try to arrange to have a private chat with some of the members. Do this *before* you actually part with any subscriptions, to save you paying out to join groups that can be of no value to you.

- Also see what trade fairs and exhibitions are on that are relevant and go along. Again, introduce yourself to as many people as you can, hand out cards and get as many in return as possible.

■ Get yourself onto appropriate social networking sites and try to make connections with as many people as possible in relevant areas; they don't have to be the hiring managers, just people who might know the hiring manager, or even know who the hiring manager is!

■ Now that you have a starting point, you can begin to meet with each person and discuss their role, industry, employer and challenges. You can take an interest in them and make offerings and suggestions of the ISTATOY type, as well as the all-important element of asking for a referral to someone else in their business with whom you can 'connect'.

Read it and reap activity

Read *Brilliant Networking* by Steven D'Souza, Prentice Hall, 2010.

After you have read the book, consider what the five top learning points are for you. Make a note of them. Write a review of the book on a book website. Plan your networking campaign and start networking.

CHAPTER 13

Wage slave or captain of your own destiny?

CAPTAIN OF YOUR DESTINY OR CAPTAIN OF INDUSTRY?

Many people dream of being their own boss, and it is important to recognise the detail in that phrase. 'Being *your own* boss' doesn't mean that you *have* to be anyone else's boss as well. Setting up your own business doesn't necessarily mean that you:

a) want to create an empire with lots of people reporting to you; nor does it mean that you

b) want to generate an enormous amount of wealth.

You may want to do one or other of these things, but not wanting to isn't a problem; unless you are going into 'the dragons' den'.

'Being your own boss' covers a huge variety of different options, and in this chapter you are encouraged to look at and think about these options and what they may mean to you and your family, and to your bank balance. Not only today, but also tomorrow and next year.

Clarifying note

For the purposes of this chapter we are going to use two pieces of shorthand:

1 'Self-employed': to mean someone who isn't working for someone else – they may be a sole trader, a partner or the director-owner of a limited company, but the important element is that they are their own boss rather than someone else's employee.

2 'PAYE': to mean that someone is employed by someone else or someone else's company or organisation.

WHY?

There are numerous reasons why you might *want* to avoid being someone else's employee, and these are just as relevant to a person starting their career as they are to someone changing career mid life, even if the 'change' is simply from PAYE to self-employed:

■ to have the freedom to choose whether you have to travel as part of your job;

■ to have the freedom to exploit an idea, invention or skill for solely your own benefit rather than on behalf of an employer;

■ to have the freedom to choose when you work with regard to 'shift patterns' – for instance if you want to fit in around your partner, children or parents;

■ to have the freedom to choose when you work with regard to seasons – for example to fit in with a sporting training schedule or a hobby;

- to have the freedom to choose how much you work, with regard to the number of hours a week.

In some types of business it is almost impossible to get a PAYE role, such as writing books, so it may not be a case of wanting to avoid being an employee but rather having to be self-employed!

CONSEQUENCES AND IMPLICATIONS

It is important to recognise that your aim is to have the 'freedom to choose' in all these cases, but freedom comes with responsibility:

- you take the responsibility for ensuring that you earn enough money for your needs, today and tomorrow;
- you take the responsibility for ensuring an income if you are sick;
- you take on the responsibility for preparing for your retirement;
- you take on the responsibility for your own health and safety;
- you take on the responsibility for your own tax liability;
- you take on the responsibility for your own development and learning.

All these responsibilities are taken (to some degree or other) by an employer if you have a PAYE job but they are part and parcel of your daily grind if you are self-employed.

THE ONLY WAY . . . ?

It may be that you don't actively *want* to be self-employed but feel that it is the lesser of two evils, the line of least resistance, or even the only viable option:

- if family commitments take you to a location where a PAYE job just isn't available;
- if family commitments require you to be available for periods of time that make it near impossible to hold down a PAYE job;
- if there is something on your CV/in your history (or missing from it) that puts off potential PAYE employers – for instance, having a criminal conviction can make it very hard to land certain jobs, having no experience can be a major hurdle, being a second-career starter can put people off (you'd be older than your boss's parents!) . . . these may not be 'right' or fair, but they are facts of life. Your choices may be to lie (as did T.E. Lawrence), to remain unemployed or to set up on your own; people seldom ask for your full history when you are a supplier rather than an employee;
- if the economy is so bad that you can get some work but not a full-time job;
- if you already have a PAYE job but want to branch out and test the waters in a new field;
- if you are entering into a career/discipline where pretty much everyone is self-employed, such as acting or individual sports;

- if you find yourself in that strange bit of accounting logic where your employer wants to make your job redundant but then hire you back as a 'consultant' for a higher daily rate, so they can move the cost of benefitting from your services from one budget to another.

OPTIONS

First, let's just look at the potential choices available to you if you want to work for yourself rather than having a PAYE job working for someone else. Note we are not looking at the different legal 'trading styles' of sole trader, partnership and limited company, but at the options for the actual finding and delivery of paying work.

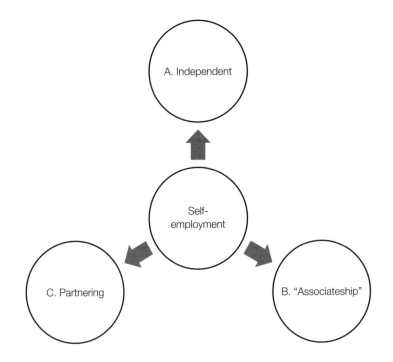

A As an independent you work pretty much alone, at least for most of the time; an example might be an artisan tradesman, a writer or a bookkeeper. You cover the entire gamut of all the activities required to run your business: you market, you sell, you do the paying work, you submit all the invoices and collect the money.

B As an 'associate' you may work for one or several organisations in the same or related work area/discipline. You are working on their behalf and under their banner. Examples are tradesmen in the construction industry, trainers working for an academy, computer programmers on contracts or consultants working for a consultancy. You often have no need to get involved in the marketing, selling or credit control elements; these are done by the organisation for which you are working. Your role is more limited to delivering the contracted service and being paid by the project or the hour/day.

C Partnering is the situation that occurs when two or more people with very similar skill sets come together for two purposes: to share the burden of marketing and accounting and to allow them together to take on larger projects than either could alone.

Many people successfully move back and forth between the three on a weekly basis – doing some of their work as an independent under their own name and charging a higher level of fee for their work (as there is no 'middle-man'), while also filling in with associateship work, which is often less well paid but has no great commitment to lead time and marketing. Then they have a 'little black book' of contacts and will form a temporary alliance with some acquaintances to exploit any opportunity of which they become aware.

It is also possible to have a 'portfolio'-style business: doing different things for different clients or in different seasons. We are not talking about normal seasonal differences but, for instance, a car mechanic who also works as a photographer, or a management trainer who also makes and sells novelty cakes, or a computer analyst who also runs several buy-to-let properties as a landlord.

Working alone

Many people set up a 'lifestyle business'; in other words, they become self-employed solely with a view to supporting their own lifestyle choice. Normally, people who go into this form of self-employment do so for the personal choices it gives them rather than the money they can make. Lifestyle businesses are generally low-cost start-ups, simply because no banker or business angel can see an adequate return on investment to lend money or buy equity in the business. Lifestyle businesses range in type from the journeyman 'artisanal' type of business, such as window cleaners or seamstresses, through to the 'special interest' type of business, such as classic car restoration or after-dinner speakers, through to the 'professional', such as a one-man-band architect or dentist, or to the 'artistic', such as painters or potters.

On the plus side, a lifestyle business usually has relatively low overheads; you're not pulled away from the work you love/are good at in order to deal with recruitment, people-management or complex stuff such as payrolls.

On the minus side, you are the sole person responsible for the selling, doing, billing, credit controlling and tax-paying. It can be a lonely existence if you aren't actively networking a lot of the time. You can be so busy delivering that you have no time to find new work to fill the diary when the current work runs out. Your business is never going to become a valuable commodity – selling up at retirement is seldom an option because *you* are the business; so if you aren't there, the business has virtually no value.

Running a lifestyle business is seldom done for the money; it is usually done for the love of the work or the love of other things in life and the work is just there to support that. Do you remember those surveys mentioned in Chapter 7?

- Interestingly, a recent survey for the insurance company Aviva suggests that over and above the 62,000 men who are actually 'economically inactive' there are a further 1.4 million men who are the main homemaker by dint of being self employed and working from home.
- Nearly half of stay-at-home mothers are running small businesses on the internet.

Be aware that many people who have set up a lifestyle business based on a hobby or interest later find that the hobby loses its shine when they have to do it 40 hours a week or to someone else's exacting standards. To paraphase the song lyrics,

> Take two-hundred-and-seventy-six! Good Lord, this used to be fun!

Or to put it in a more businesslike fashion:

> *"Find something you like, learn as much as you can about it, then decide if you like it too much to do it for a living."*
> JOHN WILSON, TRAINING MANAGER.

Many people who are successful in a lifestyle business then become unhappy when their success means that they end up employing other people to do the actual work that they loved and find themselves solely involved in the selling and managing. So remember the wisdom from Thailand, where the word *ngaan* means both 'to work' and 'to have fun'.

Working with others

Whether you set up as a formal legal partnership or a limited company, the point here is that you are sharing the load and dividing the cost of running a business. Thus, this has all the benefits of the lifestyle business, but you swap some of the headache responsibilities for the potential headaches of a falling out with your partner.

If your business partner is your life partner (what used to be called your spouse) you will both have to be prepared for the challenges of working together as well as living together. If you are aiming to set up with a person who will be solely a business partner then where will you work? On whose territory? If you want or need to go for neutral ground then you are going to incur overheads.

Becoming a 'captain of industry'

If you want to set up a company in order to generate wealth, rather than as a vehicle for you to practise a particular role, then you will need a number of skills or strategies that are less required in either of the above options:

- You will need to be able to recruit people to work for you. Sadly, this is not a natural intuition we all have, it is a skill that needs to be learned.

- You will need to be able to manage the people who work for you. This sounds easy, but it means that you have to be prepared to trust them (remembering that they are guaranteed an income, while you only get what is left after they and all the other costs have been paid).

- You are going to have to learn to trust people whom you employ; either because you have employed them to use skills and knowledge you don't have or because they can pick up work that you don't have the time to do.

- You are going to have to move away from the 'doing' and get increasingly tied up in managing the company, schmoozing customers, creditors and investors and spending more of your time slaving over a hot spreadsheet.

- Ultimately you are going to need an 'exit strategy' – a way in which you can get your just deserts out of the business and retire or move on.

TIME FOR SOME SERIOUS THINKING!

There are some questions to ask yourself before you decide to try and go it alone/set up your own business rather than finding/staying in a PAYE job. As you look at each of these questions, recognise that you may have two answers: the quick 'off the top of your head' response, and the 'now that I've looked into it and done some research' response.

1 Are you planning the move because of what going self-employed offers or to avoid what a PAYE role inflicts? If the latter, are you sure that you have looked at the fire you are getting into when you jump out of the frying pan?

2 Do you plan to work predominantly in your past industry/ discipline or a single area of interest? In either case, what differentiates you from your competitors; what is your unique selling point/proposition?

3 How much real market research have you done? What sort of number of customers are there in the relevant geographic area? What sort of prices could these customers afford to pay? Whom will you be competing with and what charges are being made by these competitors?

4 What are the pay rates/charges that you can make in comparison to your competitors? Do these match up to your income needs? Not trying to be insulting, but for many self-employed roles you can only expect to actually be doing paid work for 120 days per year . . . a PAYE role is for c. 225 days per year. So you need a day rate of almost twice your PAYE day rate just to stay vaguely in the same arena.

5 How *reliable* are your income streams going to be? There are many industries that are highly susceptible to external factors; these range from the weather, to the economy, to the competition, to outsourcing, to fashion and fad. It could be about volume (how many customers you serve) or price (how much you earn from each customer).

6 How long can you trade before you need to see money flowing into your pockets? Different business ideas and different business models have different requirements for upfront investment. They also all have varying lead times between marketing and sales, and sales and income. Have you thought about these and worked out whether you have a viable strategy? (With regard to this aspect, and that of point 4, 52 per cent of people who would like to go self-employed don't for fear that they won't earn enough money.[1])

7 If you need to raise funds, what source are you going to use? Savings if you have them; 'family, friends and fools' (there are pros and cons here!); a bank loan (has to be repaid regardless of success or failure, usually also has to be secured, generally against your home; how does your

[1] Ref: Kelly Global Workforce Index survey 2010.

spouse feel about that?); a business angel (potentially a very good source of answers to 13, 18 and 19 below, but you will a) have to be in possession of a really good business idea and b) usually have to give away a pretty large percentage of the equity, which can be very painful.)

8 Are you administratively self-sufficient (skill, equipment, space)? There is little chance of success if you cannot do the paperwork as well as the job; many an artisan, artist and technical specialist has been busy but unsuccessful because they cannot get contracts right, cannot collect money owed or cannot balance their books.

9 How does your life partner/spouse/family feel about it all? It is almost impossible to be successful in self-employment if you get a negative attitude at home; you will need to take calls out of hours, you may have to rely on your partner answering phone calls for you. You may have to work over weekends or during holidays and you may be pitched into working 12 hours a day, seven days a week. Yes, you get all the rewards of the work but some of this work is going to be speculative, i.e. you may not actually earn *anything* for it. Is your spouse going to be polite to irate/insulting/complaining/late-paying customers? This is obviously even more of a concern if you are likely to have customers visiting you at your home!

10 How healthy is your 'prospect' network? You are going to find it hard to rely on cold selling, even if you are one of the few people in the world who actually likes cold selling!

11 How will you keep your network going when you are self-employed? This again is an administrative-type function, as in point 6; some people just aren't good at it. If you are working in an 'associate' capacity you may find that the organisation you are working for deliberately tries to keep you away from networking with the decision-makers in *their* clients, understandably; they are concerned that you will undercut and poach their business away from them . . . which brings us on to . . .

12 What terms will you demand to do 'associate' work? Some organisations are flexible and will negotiate day rates on an individual basis, others just have a fixed offering: take it or leave it! Some insist on exclusivity: 'You work for us and none of our competitors!' Others are less rigid.

13 How good are you at working without the support of a team? On two levels: practical (can you do everything yourself or will you struggle?) and emotional (it can be very lonely when you have no one to chat with!) (Again the Kelly Global Workforce Index reported that 20 per cent of people who wanted to go self-employed didn't do so due to the lack of support.)

14 What will you do if you find a project that is too big for you alone? Will you build a 'virtual capability' of a network of trusted helpers whom you can call on when needed, or will you stick to doing what you can personally guarantee? What are the consequences of each course of action, and are you happy to accept them?

15 Would you consider a part-time, interim or full-time role if offered one? On what terms? This is a good test of your level of commitment to being self-employed.

16 What factors would change your current thought processes? A change in your family circumstances, a change in your health (permanent or temporary), a change in your level of experience, expertise or reputation, simply the passage of time, a change in the economy, or a change in the industry? This is especially relevant if you are thinking of going self-employed as the lesser of two evils, the line of least resistance or even the only viable option, as mentioned at the beginning of this chapter.

17 Where is this going to lead? Could you get back into corporate employment, if you wanted to, at some stage in the future? Or will you become too out-of-date/insular?

18 To whom will you turn for technical advice? In a corporate role you usually have a boss or a training department or a technical department; as a self-employed person you will have none of these people to hand. You will not be able to call IT when your PC develops the 'blue screen of death', and pension funds can be a nightmare, even if you do understand them.

19 To whom will you turn for business and management advice? OK, you may be the best mechanic in the land, the greatest artist, playwright, architect or dentist, but do you know how to raise finance, complete a VAT return or factor your debtors' book to ease cash flow? Are you *au fait* with liability legislation with regard to public liability or employer's liability or professional liability? Do you know enough about recruitment to get the right people and not end up in a tribunal over a lack of knowledge of anti-discrimination law?

20 To whom will you turn for moral support? We all have bad days, and when we do we need a supporting friend to tell our woes to and to listen to our worries. Have you got at least one 'supportive friend'?

21 How will you trade? There are advantages and disadvantages of 'Limited status' as well as sole trader and partnerships; getting it right at the outset can save a load of heartache and time later. In some industries customers won't do business with sole traders but only with limited companies or limited liability partnerships.

22 How appropriate is your personal image and does it matter to your proposed business? If it matters and it is inappropriate, how will you change it to prevent it from damaging your chances of success? And to make it beneficial to your business marketing?

Read it and reap activity

Read Dragons' Den, *Start Your Own Business, From Idea to Income*, Collins, 2010 by, well, me! After you have read the book, ask yourself how much you want to start your own business. Ask yourself how well to start your own business. Ask yourself how well suited you think you are to start your own business. Ask yourself if you intend to start your own business and if so, when? And, if you like it, write a nice review on Amazon!

YOU ARE NOT ALONE!

Here are some resources/organisations that may help you both to make a decision about becoming self-employed and as support when you are there:

The Prince's Trust **www.princes-trust.org.uk** – provides advice and grants for people under the age of 25.

Prime (The Prince's Initiative for Mature Enterprise) **www.prime.org.uk** – offers free information, workshops and business networking events. It can refer people to accredited advisers for free business advice, and in some parts of the country can also offer free mentoring and other services.

Chamber of Commerce **www.britishchambers.org.uk** – local chambers offer a range of services, from networking meetings to mentoring and business advice to formal training events.

British Business Angels Association **www.bbaa.org.uk** – is the national association dedicated to promoting angel investing and support for entrepreneurs; their members abide by a code of conduct and they also provide support in finding appropriate professional advisers.

Business Link **www.businesslink.gov.uk/bdotg/action/home** – provides local practical advice for start-ups and existing businesses on finance and grants, employing staff, taxation and much more.

Guild of Master Craftsmen **www.guildmc.com** – promotes and supports appropriate businesses and sets standards of quality and customer care.

Women & Manual Trades (**www.wamt.org**) – helps women to get into and stay in manual trades, including setting up their own business.

TIMING

Is there a right time of your life to go self-employed?

The short answer is that it all depends on a range of factors:

CASE STUDIES

John had been a mechanic for several years when he decided to go self-employed. He built a successful little business and ran it at a consistent profit for 15 years. As he approached his mid 40s he decided that the time had come to try to downshift a bit and let other people worry about the cash-flow, the bank rate, the legal liability and the staff. He sold the business and got a PAYE job where he was appreciated for his technical knowledge and his commercial acumen.

Jean had been a company-woman all her career to date. She had learnt a huge amount through both formal in-career education and by exposure to a wide range of challenging situations and environments. As she approached her mid 40s she felt that she had amassed enough credibility and contacts to stand alone as an industry expert, so she mothballed her company pension fund, took out a small bank loan and set up her own consultancy. She loved the challenge and the freedom that she had now that she was released from the strait-jacket of corporate and office politics.

Jane had been a loyal employee of a company for 12 years, but when she started a family she decided that she no longer wanted to work 45-hour weeks or to have to travel at the beck and call of her bosses and clients. She started to plan her new self-employed role as soon as she became pregnant and knew her departure date from her employer. By the time she reached the 'back-to-work' stage of motherhood she already had work lined up that provided her with intellectual stimulus, continued career development and some income for three days a week.

The 'right time' to go it alone or set up a business is the time when:

- you have really thought it all through;
- you have considered all the consequences and the implications;
- you have decided that this is the best course of action;
- you have written a proper business plan;
- you have secured adequate finance to cover all the foreseeable risks;
- you have the blessing and support of your family;
- you have a feeling of trepidation, but this is balanced by confidence in your planning and your abilities.

Don't suffer from 'paralysis by analysis'; do the research, do the maths and then get on and *do it!*

Bibliography

1 Steven Covey: *The 7 Habits of Highly Effective People* (London: Simon & Schuster, 1989).

2 See **http://top7business.com/?Top-7-Ways-To-Lock-In-Your-Legacy&id=70** for Chris Widener's article about life legacies.

3 See **http://cdn.sidsavara.com/wp-content/uploads/2008/09/researchsummary2.pdf** for a study showing the value of *writing down* goals rather than just thinking of them.

4 Margot Morrell and Stephanie Capparell: *Shackleton's Way: Leadership lessons from the great Antarctic explorer* (London: Nicholas Brealey, 2001).

5 See **http://news.bbc.co.uk/1/hi/programmes/more_or_less/5176698.stm** for the BBC story about proving 'six degrees of separation'.

6 See **http://www.guardian.co.uk/technology/2008/aug/03/internet.email** for the story relating to Microsoft's analysis regarding 'six degrees of separation'.

7 Colin Powell: *My American Journey* (New York: Ballantine, 1995).

8 Lynda Gratton: *The Shift: The future of work is already here* (London: HarperCollins, 2011).

9 Charles J. Sykes: *Dumbing Down Our Kids: Why American children feel good about themselves, but can't read, write, or add* (New York: St Martin's Press, 1995).

Glossary

Affluence trap – having all the material appearance of being rich but actually being trapped into having to pay for it all.

Brand ambassador – a person who is selected by an organisation to actively promote their brand.

Business angel – high net-worth individual who invests their own money in an entrepreneurial enterprise and often provides advice as well.

Ego – the sense of self of an individual in relation to others.

Eulogy – a laudatory speech or written tribute, especially one praising someone who has died.

Exit strategy – A plan to extricate yourself from a situation; in the context of this book the plan you have *before* you reach the point of exit, to make your transition as smooth as possible. An entrepreneur needs an exit strategy to allow them to retire and extricate the money; a person in a long-term career needs an exit strategy to change roles.

Lifestyle business – a business that never intends to grow beyond providing for the lifestyle of the proprietor.

Malapropism – the unintentional misuse of a word by confusion with one of similar sound, as in 'The sceptre of unemployment stalks the North East' (John Prescott MP). The habit of misusing words in this manner (after Mrs *Malaprop* in Sheridan's play *The Rivals* (1775) – a character who misused words).

Negative equity – a situation that arises when the value of your possessions is less than the outstanding debt you owe on them.

Prospect – in this instance a person or organisation who or that has been identified as a prospective customer.

Self-esteem – respect for or opinion of yourself.

Social network site – web-based services that allow you to: (a) construct a public or semi-public profile within certain parameters; (b) create a list of other users with whom you share a connection; and (c) view your list of connections and those made by others.

USP – unique selling point or proposition; that which differentiates you from your competitors.

Velvet rut – a situation or circumstance that you can't get out of simply because it is too comfortable.

VOIP – voice over internet protocol – making phone calls via the internet; usually free or very cheap for long international calls.

Webinar – a web seminar; the facility that allows up to several hundred people to attend a virtual seminar from their own location via the internet.

Index

accents 71, 76
accountancy 29, 84, 85
achievements 132–3, 135, 136
actors 43, 182
acupressure 143
administration skills 191
adult education courses 161,
    166, 168
advertising, careers in 29
affiliates 175
'affluence trap' 110–11, 199
Akabusi, Kriss 77
altruism 147–54
anti-abortionists 20
Argyris, Chris 155
Armed Forces 83, 85, 115
associateship 184–5, 192

bailiffs 83
banking 82
Bauby, Jean-Dominique 119
benefits packages 38, 107
Benn, Tony 77
Bezos, Jeff 68
Blair, Tony 9
Bloch, Deborah 66
blogging 102–3, 104
books, learning from 160
brand 67–80
  importance of 67–70
  maintaining your brand image
    78–80
  names 77
  rebranding yourself 75–6
  understanding your brand image
    70–4

'brand ambassadors' 108, 199
Branson, Richard 70
British Business Angels
    Association 195
The Bucket List (film) 16
Burns, Robert 69
business angels 191, 195, 199
business cards 71, 103, 133
Business Link 195

caffeine 143, 145
Caine, Michael 134–5
'calling cards' 103, 117, 177–8
'captains of industry' 188
carbohydrates 144
career planning ix
catering 82–3
Chamber of Commerce 195
charity 108, 147, 148–52
children 81, 86, 87
  cost of raising 83
  dependence on current career
    107
  developmental stages 94–5
  emotional legacy left to 10–11
  relocation impact on 110
  self-esteem 125, 126–7
  work/life balance 60
  see also family
Chilton, David 13
chocolate 142
Christensen, Clayton M. 146, 164
Churchill, Winston 7, 15, 166
civil engineering 84
co-workers, relationships with 40
'communities of practice' 164

community organisations 109, 149
contacts 41, 102
    networking 49–51, 103, 104,
        118, 176–8, 191–2
    personal contact books 117–18
covering letters 72
Covey, Stephen 6
criticism, giving too much 125–6,
        127–8
customers, relationships with 40
CVs 71, 117, 133, 182
cynicism 19

danger 40, 83
delegation of work 42
Deming, W. Edwards 158
Diana, Princess of Wales 7
diet 142, 144–5
documentation 71–2
Douglas, Kirk 77
'downsizing' 111
Draco 15
'Dress for Success' 140
D'Souza, Steven 178
Dyno-Rod 41

ego 117, 121–46
    definition of 122, 199
    helping others 138–9
    'little voice' in your head 128
    physical appearance 139–41
    pride in what you do 134–5
    pride in your achievements
        132–3
    scale of self-interest 122–3
    success and failure 129–32
    transferable skills 136–8
    see also self-esteem
Einstein, Albert 16
Elizabeth II, Queen of England 1
Elton, Ben 76
emails 174
emotional legacies 10–11
employability x
essential oils 143
ethical legacies 11

eulogies 6, 7, 199
exercise 141–2
existence, reason for 5–6
exit strategy 97, 188, 199
expatriates 105
experience, learning from 158,
        159, 164, 167

Facebook 72, 118, 152, 173
failure 124, 129–32
family
    as a career 89–97
    career compatibility with 81–7
    as co-workers 114
    dependence on current career
        107
    emotional legacy left to 10–11
    importance of xii–xiii
    influence on self-esteem 125,
        126–7
    questions to ask yourself 85–7
    reasons for self-employment 182
    relocation impact on 110
    skills 137–8
    values 17
    work/life balance 53, 54, 60,
        63, 65
family trees 14
financial legacies 12–13
Ford, Henry 124
Friends Reunited 72, 173
The Full Monty (film) 111
funds, raising 191
funeral, imagining your own 6–8
future-proofing your career 99–120
    getting the most from the
        present 101–4
    personal capacity 112–13
    against redundancy 117–19
    'velvet rut' 104–10
    wants 99–101

Gandhi, Mahatma 158
Gates, Bill 163
genealogy 14
goals xiii, 1–5, 16, 108

Gratton, Lynda 118, 119
Grylls, Bear 73
Guild of Master Craftsmen 195

hairdressing 84
Halvorson, Heidi 157
happiness
    future-proofing your career
        108–9, 112–13
    sacrificing 37
    self-esteem linked to 139
    work/life balance 58–64, 65
head-hunters 118
health 12, 65, 144, 165
helping others 138–9, 152–4
Hertzberg, Frederick 33
Hill, Harry 101
hobbies 109, 186–7
holidays 63, 145, 165
homemakers 89–97, 186
    career phases 94–5
    questions to ask yourself 96–7
    responsibilities of 92–3
    transferable skills 137–8
hours of work *see* working hours
humanism 3

illness 119
image consultants 78
image, publicising your 171–6
    see also brand
intangible likes 39–41
intellectual legacies 13–14
internet
    blogging 102–3, 104
    learning from the 161–2, 163,
        164, 166
    stay-at-home mothers 94, 186
    see also websites
ISTATOYs (I Saw This And Thought
    Of You) 174–5, 178

job descriptions 31, 44–8
job security 83, 115
job titles, defining yourself by 135
Johnson, Spencer 120

Keillor, Garrison 8
kindness, random acts of 138–9,
    152–4
Kiyosaki, Robert T. 13

language
    learning a new 165
    use of 71, 75
'learned dependence' 126
learning 103, 109, 155–69
    funding your 168–9
    intentional 159–64
    intuitive 158–9
    methods of 166–7
    reasons for 165–6
    when and where to learn 167
    work/life balance 61
legacy, leaving a 9–16
leisure activities 53, 56, 60
life goals 1–5, 16
life phases 100–1
'lifestyle businesses' 185–7, 199
light, exposure to 142
likes and dislikes 33–52, 100–1
    assessing your 38–41
    finding the 'right' career 44–9
    listing your 42
    networking 49–51
    scenarios 42–3
    WAGs 37
limited companies 187, 194
LinkedIn 72, 118, 152, 173
'little voice' in your head 128
location of work 39, 42
'locus of control' 130–1
love, giving too much 125–7
Luddites 15

Madonna 77
magazines 161, 174
Magnanti, Brooke 102
management consultancy 83
Maslow, Abraham 33
material likes 38, 51–2
Maxwell, Robert 114
media 17, 18, 19

meetings 159–60
men, as homemakers 90, 186
mentors 163, 166
Milgram, Stanley 49
Minder (TV show) 38
mission statements 20, 29
money 48–9, 52, 63
    dangerous work 40
    homemakers 96
    police officers 47
    self-employment 189–91
    supporting a family 83
    'velvet ruts' 107
Mr T. 146
musicians 43
MySpace 118

names 73, 77
Nazism 20
needs 33
networking 49–51, 103, 104, 118,
        176–8, 191–2
    see also social networking sites
not-for-profit (NFP) organisations
        148–52

oil and gas industry 43
Open University 162, 163
out-of-hours working 59

parents, looking after 81, 87, 96
partnering 184, 187
PAYE 180, 181, 182, 190
personal capacity 99, 112–13
personality traits 20–3
philanthropy 108
photographs 72
physical appearance 68–70, 78,
        139–41
physical job demands 112, 113
physical legacies 12
Picasso, Pablo 165
pictorial records 102, 104, 132
police officers 44–8
portfolio of careers 115
Powell, Colin 62, 117

praise 125, 126
prejudices 74–5
pride
    happiness with work 62
    status likes 39
    in your achievements 132–3, 135
    in yourself 134
Prime (The Prince's Initiative for
        Mature Enterprises) 195
The Prince's Trust 195
professional associations 109,
        152, 177
promotions 172
prospects 191, 200
public relations (PR) 171–6
public sector workers 107

qualifications 109, 133, 134,
        163, 167

random acts of kindness 152–4
recruitment advertisements 29–30,
        74, 118
redundancy ix–x, 114, 115, 116,
        117–19
reflective thinking xvii–xviii
relationships with co-workers 40
religion 2, 20
relocating for work 42, 83, 86, 110
reputation 41, 118
retail 82, 84, 114
retirement 112, 113
Richmond, Lee 66
risk management 31
Roosevelt, Eleanor 146
Roosevelt, Franklin D. 7
Ross, Harold 105
routines, varying your 144

salaries *see* money
Seal 77
secondments 86
self-coaching xvi
self-employment 51, 179–97
    associateship 184–5, 192
    'captains of industry' 188

definition of 180
male homemakers 90, 186
questions to ask yourself 188–94
reasons for being 180–1
responsibilities of 181–2
sources of information 195
timing 196–7
work/life balance 56
working alone 184, 185–7
working with others 185, 187
self-esteem 103, 123–4, 146
definition of 200
helping others 138–9
'locus of control' 130
physical appearance and 139–41
pride in your achievements 132,
133, 135
tiredness 141
transferable skills 136, 138
volunteering 150
'self-fulfilling prophecy' 124
self-interest 122–3
'seven point plan' 10
Seymour, Jane 77
Shackleton, Ernest 136
shift work 48, 82–3
Simpson, Homer 158
single-employment careers 113–14
'six degrees of separation' 49
skills
administration 191
homemakers 92–3, 137–8
learning new 109, 157, 164, 165
transferable 104, 136–8
volunteering 149–50
Slater, Lucinda 79
sleep 145
smell, sense of 143
social networking sites 72, 118,
173, 178, 200
The Sound of Music (film) 52
spiritual legacies 11
sportspeople 43, 83, 182
spouses and partners 81, 84–5, 97
dependence on current career
107

emotional legacy left to 10–11
relocation impact on 110
self-employment impact on
191–2
see also family
status likes 39
'stuck in a rut' situations 104–10
success and failure 124, 129–32,
136
supportive friends xiii–xvi, 193
Sykes, Charles J. 19

teachers 18, 125, 126
tiredness 141–5
Toksvig, Sandi 76
tone of voice 71
Townsend, Pete 8
trade associations 109, 177
trade fairs and exhibitions 177–8
training 41, 109, 150, 157
transferable skills 104, 136–8
Twitter 72, 161, 173

unemployment 116, 140
see also redundancy
unique selling point/proposition
(USP) 189, 200
University of the Third Age (U3A)
166

values 17–31, 108–9
brand 74
career choices 28–31
influences on 18–19
personal value statement 23
personality traits 20–3
ranking your 24–6
scenarios 27–8
sources of 17
status likes 39
strongly held 19–20
WAGs 36
Vega, Lizandra 78
'velvet rut' 104–10, 200
voice, tone of 71

voicemail 72, 173
volunteering 60, 148–52, 164

WAGs (Wives And Girlfriends) 34–7
wants 99–101
Webb, Liggy 66, 73, 139
webinars 94, 161–2, 200
websites
   career listings 44
   'careers' pages on company
      websites 74
   company values 29
   learning from 161
   social networking sites 72, 118,
      173, 178, 200
   see also internet
weight, maintaining a healthy 145
Weston, Simon 119
The Who 8
Who Do You Think You Are? (TV
   show) 14

Widener, Chris 10, 11
Women & Manual Trades 195
women, as homemakers 90, 186
Wooster, Bertie 158
work environment 40, 47
work/life balance 48, 53–66
   adjusting your 65–6
   happiness element 58–64
   questions to ask yourself 54–5,
      57, 62–4
   time element 55–7
working from home 94
working hours
   family issues 82
   likes and dislikes 40, 42, 52
   police officers 48
   self-employment 56, 181, 189–2
   shift work 48, 82–3
   'velvet ruts' 107
   work/life balance 55–7, 59
The Wright Stuff (TV show) 37